ENGLISH-OLD ENGLISH, OLD ENGLISH-ENGLISH DICTIONARY

Edited by

GREGORY K. JEMBER

with

JOHN C. CARRELL
ROBERT P. LUNDQUIST
BARBARA M. OLDS
RAYMOND P. TRIPP, JR.

•WESTVIEW PRESS•BOULDER•COLORADO•

Copyright 1975 by Westview Press, Inc.

Published 1975 in the United States of America by

Westview Press, Inc.
1898 Flatiron Court
Boulder, Colorado 80301
Frederick A. Praeger, Publisher and Editorial Director

Printed in the United States of America

Library of Congress Cataloging in Publication Data

Jember, Gregory K
    English-Old English and Old English-English
dictionary.

    1. Anglo-Saxon language--Dictionaries--English.
2. English language--Dictionaries--Anglo-Saxon.
I. Title.
PE279.J4   429'.3'21   75-30928
ISBN 0-89158-006-9

For

Harold M. Priest

Bocere, Lareow, and Freond

This dictionary answers the need for a reference
tool and pedagogical aid that will enable the student to write simple Old English and thus gain
an active and creative command of this earliest
stage of our language. Nearly 5,000 of the most
common words, conveniently alphabetized in each
section, provide a basic vocabulary that meets the
needs of elementary composition and translation.
The dictionary also contains a linguistic introduc-
tion that provides an outline grammar: common
inflections, connectives, prepositions, affixes for
fashioning new compounds, and an essential sum-
mary of syntactical patterns and the use of cases.

Gregory Jember received his doctorate from the
University of Denver, where he specialized in Old
English language and literature; he has also writ-
ten on Shakespeare and edited *Essays in Litera-
ture*. He taught in the English department at the
University of Denver, and is at present with the
University of Colorado. Mr. Jember's co-editors
are connected with the University of Denver.

PREFACE

This modern English-Old English-modern English dictionary is the first double entry dictionary available to students of Old English. It is intended to be a practical instrument towards the improvement of the teaching of Old English. Beginning students learn, at best, to read Old English with some fluency, but lack the means to gain that deeper knowledge of the language that can come only from composing in it. Thus, in offering this dictionary primarily as a pedagogical aid, we hope to make it possible for the student to write simple Old English and thereby to enhance his full command of the language. We also provide a short glossary of Old English words to the beginning student whose needs are usually exceeded by presently available lexicographical sources.

Innumerable difficulties obviously arise in such an undertaking as this. The meaning of many Old English words is, to say the least, often elusive. Precise modern English equivalents are difficult to determine. Furthermore, the scope of a practicable vocabulary is not easily decided. The following remarks, however, set forth our chief editorial criteria.

VOCABULARY SELECTION

Since a prime objective is to enable students to write in Old English, what the student might wish to write about governed, for the most part, the selection of lexical items. Thus words for animals, colors, basic human activities, domestic items, natural phenomena, time, etc. are included. In some instances, we have ventured to reconstruct Old English forms which do not appear in either the poetic or prose corpus, but for which the student may have use. Likely enough, every teacher of Old English will have his own priorities for what constitutes an essential vocabulary for beginning students so that the present selection may not entirely meet every instructional need. We can say only that our own judgments and priorities are reflected in the vocabulary presented here.

DEFINITIONS

In general, we have not sought to provide new definitions for Old English words and have instead most often retained conventional definitions, since   (1) it was not our purpose to provide a new dictionary of Old English, and (2) such a work is already in preparation. However, when, in the opinion of the editors, a conventional definition was considered to be inaccurate, deficient, or less specific than present knowledge allows, we have then supplied qualification or redefined the word.

ORTHOGRAPHY

As a consequence of the exigencies of production, some of the orthographic conventions normally associated with the transcription of Old English have not been employed. The "ash" is printed with two letters without ligature (*ae*); the "yogh" is printed as *g*; and "eth" (*ð*, *Ð*) is consistently used to represent both "thorn" and "eth."

NORMALIZATION

The question of normalization is a difficult one. Since the texts themselves evidence mixed forms, complete normalization to any one date or dialect must be regarded as involving questionable artificiality. Generally, we have selected forms from the literary koine, the dialect the beginning student would be most likely to know. But a number of early and alternate forms are also included. When, for example, sound changes have obscured the morphology of a compound, we have often preferred the earlier form, e.g., *wiohbed* in preference to *weofod*. Such eclecticism in providing a range of forms should give students a more accurate picture of the realities of Old English and of language itself.

ALPHABETIZATION OF ENTRIES

Entries are arranged alphabetically, with *ae* following *a*, and *ð* following *t*. Old English words normally beginning with a prefix are alphabetized according to the prefix and not the stem. Alternative spellings, indicated parenthetically, as in *me(o)du*, do not alter alphabetic order.

DESIGN OF THE DICTIONARY

No attempt has been made to achieve complete cross-reference. If a student cannot find the particular word he needs under one entry, he should think of modern English synonyms and then look again.

Main entries are printed in capital letters. When a particular form falls into more than one lexical category, we have usually followed a noun, verb, adjective, adverb order. Additional specification is provided only when confusion seems likely. The appearance of a symbol for gender, for example, obviates the necessity of a symbol for noun; likewise, the number of a verb class obviates the necessity of a symbol for verb.

The arrangement of information included with Old English nouns and verbs is as follows:

1. Nouns: Old English entry; plural form(s)—where given—in parentheses; gender(s).

2. Verbs: Old English entry; class(es). Classes of weak verbs are indicated by lower case Roman numerals (i-iii); classes of strong verbs by Arabic numerals (1-7). Mixed forms are also indicated.

Connotative values are generally not listed, although parenthetical qualification is occasionally provided beside the modern English entry.

Long and short values are not distinguished.

(Additional information and directions are given in the syntactical section of the dictionary.)

OTHER FEATURES

For the sake of quick reference, an outline grammar listing essential paradigms is included. Since the student will most likely have a complete Old English grammar available to him and an instructor who can assist him, no attempt has been made to be exhaustive.

A section on word formation and syntax follows the grammar.

Finally, we wish to emphasize that this dictionary has been prepared for the beginning student and has therefore been kept intentionally free from highly technical language and a bulky scholarly apparatus. Our criterion has been accurate, useful simplicity. The advanced student who requires highly detailed lexicographical, grammatical, or syntactical information should of course consult the appropriate specialized works.

My associate editors and I are deeply grateful for the assistance of Professor Stuart B. James, Chairman, Department of English, and the support of the Graduate School of Arts and Sciences, University of Denver, in providing a research grant which enabled us to have the final manuscript typed and thus to complete the project on schedule.

University of Denver   G. K. J.
Denver, Colorado
September 1975

TABLE OF ABBREVIATIONS

a	adjective
acc	accusative
anv	anomalous verb
av	adverb
conj	conjunction
dat	dative
f	feminine
gen	genitive
ins	instrumental
m	masculine
n	neuter
neg	negative
nom	nominative
ns	noun/substantive
nv	noun derived from verb
part	particle
pl	plural
pp	past participle
pr	pronoun
pref	prefix
prep	preposition
pres	present
prp	preterite present
sg	singular
st	strong
suff	suffix
v	verb
va	adjective derived from verb (verbal adjective)
vn	verb derived from noun
wk	weak
1	highest frequency
2	very frequent
Ø	without meaning
+	various parts of speech
?	uncertain
→	gives

OUTLINE GRAMMAR

PERSONAL PRONOUNS

First Person

	Sg.	Dual	Pl.
Nom	ic	wit	we
Acc	me	unc	us
Gen	min	uncer	ure
Dat	me	unc	us

Second Person

	Sg.	Dual	Pl.
Nom	þu	git	ge
Acc	þe	inc	eow
Gen	þin	incer	eower
Dat	þe	inc	eow

Third Person

	Sg.			Pl.
	M.	N.	F.	All Genders
Nom	he	hit	heo	hie
Acc	hine	hit	hie	hie
Gen	his	his	hi(e)re	hi(e)ra
Dat	him	him	hi(e)re	him

DEFINITE ARTICLE AND DEMONSTRATIVE

	Sg.			Pl.
	M.	N.	F.	All Genders
Nom	se	þæt	seo	þa
Acc	þone	þæt	þa	þa
Gen	þaes	þaes	þaere	þara
Dat	þaem	þaem	þaere	þaem
Ins	þy	þy/þon	(þaere)	

DEMONSTRATIVE

	M.	N.	F.	All Genders
Nom	þes	þis	þeos	þas
Acc	þisne	þis	þas	þas
Gen	þisses	þisses	þisse	þissa
Dat	þissum	þissum	þisse	þissum
Ins	þys	þys	(þisse)	

INTERROGATIVE

	M. and F.	N.
Nom	hwa	hwaet
Acc	hwone	hwaet
Gen	hwaes	hwaes
Dat	hwaem	hwaem
Ins		hwy/hwon

STRONG ADJECTIVE AND NOUN TERMINATIONS

Sg.

	M. A.	M. Noun	N. A.	N. Noun	F. A.	F. Noun
Nom	—	—	—	—	—u	—u, —
Acc	—ne	—	—	—	—e	—e
Gen	—es	—es	—es	—es	—re	—e
Dat	—um	—e	—um	—e	—re	—e
Ins	—e		—e		—re	

Pl.

	M. A.	M. Noun	N. A.	N. Noun	F. A.	F. Noun
Nom	—e	—as	—u	—u, —	—a, —e	—a, —e
Acc	—e	—as	—u	—u, —	—a, —e	—a, —e
Gen	—ra	—a	—ra	—a	—ra	—a, —ena
Dat	—um	—um	—um	—um	—um	—um

WEAK ADJECTIVE AND NOUN TERMINATIONS

Sg.

	M. A.	M. Noun	N. A.	N. Noun	F. A.	F. Noun
Nom	—a	—a	—e	—e	—e	—e
Acc	—an	—an	—e	—e	—an	—an
Gen	—an	—an	—an	—an	—an	—an
Dat	—an	—an	—an	—an	—an	—an

Pl.

	M. A.	M. Noun	N. A.	N. Noun	F. A.	F. Noun
Nom	—an	—an	—an	—an	—an	—an
Acc	—an	—an	—an	—an	—an	—an
Gen	—ra, —ena	—ena	—ra, —ena	—ena	—ra, —ena	—ena
Dat	—um	—um	—um	—um	—um	—um

VERBS

Present Indicative — Personal Terminations

	Class i Wk. and St.			Class ii Wk.			Class iii Wk.	
	Sg.	Pl.		Sg.	Pl.		Sg.	Pl.
1	—e	—að	1	—ie	—iað	1	—e	—að
2	—est	—að	2	—ast	—iað	2	—ast	—að
3	—eð	—að	3	—iað	—iað	3	—að	—að

Preterite Indicative — The Gradation of Strong Verbs

Class	3 Sg. Pres.	Pret. Sg.	Pret. P.	Pp.
1	i	a	i	i
2	eo(u)	ea	u	o
3	i(e, eo)	a(ea, ea)	u(u, u)	u(o, o)
4	e(i)	ae(a)	ae(o)	o(u)
5	e(ie)	ae(ea)	ae(ea)	e(ie)
6	a	o	o	a
7	x	z	z	x

— Personal Terminations

	St.			Wk.	
	Sg.	Pl.		Sg.	Pl.
1	—	—on	1	—e	—on
2	—e	—on	2	—est	—on
3	—	—on	3	—e	—on

Present and Preterite Subjunctive — Personal Terminations

	Sg.	Pl.
1	—e	—en
2	—e	—en
3	—e	—en

Imperative

St.

Sg.	Pl.
—	—að

Wk.

	Sg.	Pl.
Class i	—e	—(i)að
Class ii	—a	—iað
Class iii	—a, —e	—að

VERBAL TERMINATIONS

Infinitive	—(i)an
Inflected Infinitive	—(i)enne
Present Participle	—(i)ende
Past Participle (Wk.):	
Class i	—ed
Class ii	—od
Class iii	—(o)d

PREPOSITIONS

Preposition	Cases	General Meanings
aefter	acc	after, according to
	dat	after, along, on account of
aet	acc	unto, up to, as far as
	dat	near, by, in, on, with
an	acc / dat	in, on, among, with respect to
and	acc	over, against, with
	dat	with (in numbers)
be	dat / ins	by, at, on, on account of
fram	dat	from, away from
	ins	away from
for	dat	above, before, instead of
geond	acc	through(out), beyond, over
in	acc	in, into, upon, up, up to
	dat	in, at, during, for
	ins	in
mid	acc / dat / ins	with, by means of, among
ofer	acc	over, up, despite
	dat	above, upon
on	acc	on, in, to, toward, upon
	dat / ins	on, upon, in
ongean	acc / dat	against, opposite
oð	acc	until, to, up to, as far as
to	acc	to, toward, at, in
	dat	to, for, during, till

þurh	acc	through, during, by means of
under	acc / dat	under, underneath, below
wið	acc	to, against, toward, beside, with, at
ymb(e)	acc	about, along, concerning
	dat	about, around, concerning

J. C. C.

WORD-FORMATION AND WORD-ORDER

WORD-FORMATION

English word formation, in any age, is a subtle business, one involving semantic and morphological patterns of the kind the native speaker comes to know unconsciously, as it were, by virtue of participating in his culture. Language and culture come so close to being "the same thing," that "thinking" and word formation also tend to coincide. It is one thing, therefore, to say (negatively): "No, *we* never say that!" and quite another thing to say positively (and ahead of time) what in fact *we* do say.

Language, if not entirely arbitrary, is, at the least, inconsistent. It is highly particular and concrete in its many "exceptions," so that it is impossible to generalize logically about what a given combination of words or combination of words, prefixes, and suffixes *ought* consistently to mean. *ShameFUL* and *shameLESS*, though to be sure via different routes, come to mean "the same thing": *disgraceful.* And many think *in*flammable substances do *not* burn! The fact is that language can never be separated from life and experience; and this means, as far as word formation goes, that the fashioning of new words cannot be reduced to so many hard and fast rules. The essential pieces of language, of course, may be provided, and their most common combinations, but still the writer coining new words or judging the acceptability of those he encounters must in the last analysis depend upon his own degree of participation in his culture-language.

Fortunately for the beginning student, the way words are put together has not changed too much from Anglo-Saxon days—the ancient Indo-European patterns still hold. Thus, in most instances, the student, in shaping *new* Old English words from items in this dictionary, can safely rely on his own contemporary word sense. Even though later borrowing from other languages has replaced many prefixes and suffixes and altered the meaning of still others, as well as increased the number and variety of the pieces of language available for affixing, the old patterns survive.

Overlooking certain subtle matters (like thematic stem vowels and inflections themselves), word formation still means primarily prefixes, suffixes, and compounds. Things like functional shift, that is, using one part of speech for another, have become more important, while gradation or changes like *sing, sang*, etc., have become less important since the Renaissance or Early Modern English Period.

Old English had its equivalent to functional shift (in the formation of weak verbs from nouns), but made heavier use of affixing and compounding.

In order to assist the student in coining new words, a few basic patterns of affixing and compounding in Old English will be pointed out.

Prefixing. Prefixes in Old English or rather prefix-word combinations present, as in modern English, many subtle variations of meaning and ways to change meaning. (This extends to the fact that a certain meaning may be achieved either through the use of a prefix or a suffix.) Basically, however, prefix-word combinations are constructed upon *three* conceptual patterns: (1) the prefix carries *adjectival* force; (2) the prefix carries *adverbial* force; or (3) the prefix carries *prepositional* force. (Stress or accent is closely connected to the semantic status of the prefix and the resulting combination.) Old English prefixes (41 are provided) are outnumbered by their modern counterparts (approximately 66). Not all Old English prefixes have, of course, survived, or survived unchanged: semantic competition, among themselves and with similar, more rational Latinate forms, loss of certain ideas and conceptual relationships, and the adoption of different patterns of word formation, have all conspired to cut their number down considerably, to about eight: *a—, be—, for—, fore—, mid—, mis—, step—, twi—, un—* (negative), *and un— (and—.* opposition).

The following list of Old English prefixes contains the most commonly used ones, some of which, of course, are also independent words in their own right. It is further a subtle matter whether or not certain words should be classed as prefixes when they are seldom used as such. The list also provides other information, such as the primary formative functions of a given prefix and the parts of speech with which it regularly combines, plus illustrative examples.

In order to assist the student in locating the most semantically appropriate prefix, a list of modern English prefixes is also provided, with the *approximate* Old English equivalents. Exact correspondence is in many cases impossible. But in searching for the most appropriate prefix in constructing a complex Old English word, the student (if he does not wish to rely upon his own linguistic intuition) may first check this modern list and then look for a "model" Old English word that exhibits a similar semantic pattern. For example, if the student wishes to construct an Old English prefix to use for the meaning of "vice," he could check this modern list and find *under—.* Then checking compounds beginning with *under—,* he would find *undercyning,* "viceroy," and thus confirm his choice.

A List of Prefixes

KEY   Abbreviations listed below in the Prefix column and the Use column
—indicating the parts of speech with which prefixes are commonly
combined—are found in the Table of Abbreviations (p. viii).

Prefix	Meaning and Function	Use	Examples
a—1	Intensification; change of durative aspect to perfective	v; vn, va ∅	*aheawan,* cut off *ahebban,* lift up *acennednes,* birth *araed,* resolute *(a)bodian,* announce
a—	"Ever"	va	*alibbende,* everlasting
a—, o—, (aeg—)	Generalization of pronouns and adverbs	pr, av	*ahwaer,* anywhere *ahwaeðer,* either (of two)
ae—	"Without"; formation of adjectives from nouns	ns	*aefelle,* without skin *aewene,* hopeless
aef— (of—)	"Off"	ns	*aefðanc(a),* grudge *aefest,* envy *aefweard,* absent
aefter—	"After"	+	*aefterfylgan,* pursue *aefterlean,* recompense
aeg— (a—, o—)	Generalization of pronouns and adverbs	pr, av	*aeghwa,* everyone *aeghwider,* in all directions
an—1, on—(un—, and—)	Inception of an action; as *un—* = inversion of meaning; as *and—* = opposition; also locative	+, ∅	*onbaernan,* set afire *onwaecnan,* wake up *on(un)lucan,* unlock *on(and)raes,* attack *onblawan,* blow on *onclifian,* stick to
and—2 (ond—)	"Against"	ns, vn; a, av	*andsaca,* adversary *ondhwearfan,* turn against *andlang,* entire *andgytfullice,* intelligently
be—1 bi—, big—	"By, over, around"; intensification; privation	v; ns, av	*bebugan,* surround *begeotan,* pour over *beswelgan,* swallow up *bifylce,* neighboring people *bedaelan,* deprive of *behadian,* unfrock
ed—	"Again, back"	+	*edcierr,* a return *edniwe,* renewed *edstaðelian,* re-establish
el—	"Foreign, from elsewhere"	+	*elðeodig,* foreign *elles,* otherwise *elcor,* elsewhere

Prefix	Meaning and Function	Use	Examples
for—1	Intensification with loss or destruction; with adjectives = very	v; a	*fordon*, destroy *forgieldan*, forfeit *foroft*, very often *forheard*, very heard
fore—	"First, foremost, before"	+	*foregan*, precede *foreðanc*, forethought *foresnotor*, most wise
forð—	"Motion toward, continuing"	+	*forðbringan*, bring forth *forðgeorn*, eager to advance *forðgang*, progress, a going forth *forthlice*, forwardly
fram—	"From"	+	*framsið*, departure *framcyme*, progeny
ful(l)—	"Completeness"	+	*fulgan*, accomplish *fulwite*, full penalty *fulneah*, almost
ge—1	"Together"; formation of perfective, resultative, and transitive verbs	v; +, ∅	*gefera*, companion *gemaecca*, mate *gesittan*, inhabit *gesceran*, cut through *gestandan*, endure, stand *gereord*, speech
geond—	"Through, throughout"; formation of perfective, intensive verbs	v	*geondwadan*, know thoroughly *geondfaran*, pervade *geonddrencan*, get drunk
in(n)—2	"In"; directional, locative; intensification (like *on—*)	+	*ingenga*, invader *inadl*, internal sickness *infrod*, very wise *indrencan*, intoxicate
mid—	"With": locative and associative; instrumental	+	*midspreca*, advocate *midwyrhta*, cooperator *midwist*, presence, company
mis—	"Amiss, wrongly"	+	*mislar*, bad teaching *misraed*, misguidance *misfon*, fail to get *mislimpan*, go wrong *miswerde*, erring, bad-behaving
of—2	Perfective intensification; with nouns *aef—*	v	*offaran*, overtake *offerian*, carry off *oftorfian*, stone to death

Prefix	Meaning and Function	Use	Examples
ofer—2	"Over, excess"; with verbs, adverbial; with nouns often pejorative	v; ns; a, +	*ofercuman*, overcome *oferhycgan*, despise *oferwreon*, cover over *ofermaegen*, superior force *oferbru*, eyebrow *oferaet*, gluttony *ofersad*, very (too) sad
on—1 *(an—)*	Inception of action	v; ns	(For verbs see *an—*.) *onbringe*, instigation *onflaescnes*, incarnation *onsting*, authority
or—	"Wanting, not having"; transformation of nouns to adjectives	ns	*orsawle*, lifeless *orsorg*, without anxiety *orðanc*, ingenious
oð—	"Away (from); at, close to	v	*oðberan*, carry off *oðwindan*, escape *oðstandan*, stand still
sam—	"Together"	ns, a	*samhiwan*, members of household *samwist*, living together *samheort*, unanimous *samwinnende*, struggling together
sam—	"Half"	a	*samworht*, half-built *samcwicu*, half-alive
sin—	"Extensive, lasting, perpetual"	+	*sinniht*, eternal night *sinscipe*, wedlock *singal*, continuous
to—2	"Motion toward, location at"; perfective (destructive) with verbs	+	*tocyme*, arrival *toweard*, toward *todaeg*, today *tobrecan*, break to pieces *tofeallan*, fall to pieces
twi—	"Two, twice, twofold"; mostly formation of adjectives from nouns	ns; a	*twibill*, two-edged sword *twifeald*, twofold *twispraece*, double tongued, false
ðri—	"Three, thrice, threefold"; mostly formation of adjectives from nouns	ns; a	*ðridaeled*, tripartite *ðridaeglic*, lasting three days *ðrisciete*, triangular
ðurh—	"Through, completely; very (with adjectives)"	v; a	*ðurhdrifan*, pierce *ðurhwunian*, persist *ðurhbeorht*, very bright

Prefix	Meaning and Function	Use	Examples
un—,1 (*an—, on—)*	"Opposite, reverse"; often intensification with pejorative implications	a, av; v (rare); ns	*unar,* dishonor *ungelic,* dissimilar *unrihte,* unjustly *unorne,* simple, humble *uncraeft,* malpractice *uncoðu,* disease *unhar,* very gray
under—	"Under, beneath, underlying"	v; ns	*underfeon,* receive *undergietan,* understand *underðeodan,* subjugate *underburg,* suburb *undercyning,* viceroy
up—	"Up, away, rising"	+	*uplang,* upright *upgang,* landing *upflering,* upper floor *upaspringan,* spring up
ut—	"Out, away"; sometimes intensification	+	*utcwealm,* utter destruction *utfus,* eager to depart, die *utlagu,* outlaw *utfaer,* exit *utlendisc,* strange, foreign
wan— (*won—)*	"Wanting, lacking, deficient"; privative and negative	ns, a	*wanhyd,* recklessness *wanhal,* sick *wanhaga,* poor person *wansceaft,* misery
wið—	"Away, against"	+	*wiðbregdan,* snatch away *wiðsacan,* oppose, deny *wiðinnan,* within *wiðsuðan,* to the south *wiðlaednes,* abduction
wiðer—	"Opposing, counter"	+	*wiðercwide,* contradiction *wiðertrod,* retreat *wiðerraede,* adverse
ymb(e)—	"Around, about"	+	*ymbespraece,* comment *ymbhycgan,* consider *ymbgang,* circumference *ymbfaer,* circuit *ymbsittan,* besiege

A List of Approximate Semantic Correspondences Between Modern and Old English Prefixes

Modern English	Old English
a— (afield)	an—, on—
a— (asymmetric)	un—
ante— (pre—)	fore—, aer—, aerne—
anti—	and— (an—), un—, wið—, wiðer—
arch—	fore—, (ful(l)—, ofer—, in—, sin— ðurh—, ut—
auto—	self—
be—	be—, bi(g)—
bi—	twi—
circum—	ymb(e)—, be—, under—
cis—	neah—, (wiðinnan, beheonan)
co—	ge—, mid—, sam—
counter—	and—, wiðer—, wið—
crypto—	under—, (dyrne, deogol)
de— (dis—, un—)	un—, and—, be—, for—, wan—, to—, fram—, niðer—, dune—
demi—	sam—, healf—
di—	twi—
dis— (de—, un—)	un—, and—, be—, for—, wan—, to—, fram—
en—, em—	in—, ymb(e)-, an—, ful—, a—, to—, under—
epi—	in—, uppan—, be—, ofer—, (a)bufan—
ex—	fram—, fore—, aer—, eald—
extra—	oðer—, ut(era)—, geond—, ðurh—, for—, el—
fore—	fore—
hyper—	ofer—, for—, ful(l)—, mis—, sin—, heah—
hypo—	wan—, or—, ae—, hean—
in— (negative)	un—, wan—, wiðer—
inter—	betwux—
intra—	innan— (wiðinnan)
mal—	un—, mis—
meta—	geond—, ut(era)—
micro—; macro—	lyt—, smael—; micel—, strang—, maegen—
mid—	mid—
mis—	mis—
mono—	an—
multi—	manig—, fela—, micel—
neo—	niw(e)—, fersc—
non—	un—, and—, ae—, or—, wan—, wiðer—, wið—
pan—	eal(l)—, sam—
para—	ymb(e)—, be—, neah—
per— (chemical)	heah—, micel—, fore—
peri—	ymb(e)—
poly—	mani—, fela—, micel—
post—	aefter—, hinder—, (hindan)

Modern English	Old English
pre—	*fore—, aer—, aerne—*
preter—	*geond—, ut(era)—*
pro— (substitute)	*under—, fostor—*
pro— (ante—, fore—, pre—)	*fore—, aer—, aerne—*
pro— (in favor of)	*freond—, leof—, freo—*
proto—	*fore—*
pseudo—	*leas—, un—*
re—	*ed—*
retro—	*ed—, hinder—*
semi—	*sam—, healf—, neah—*
step—	*steop—*
sub—	*under—, niðer—*
super—	*ofer—, geond—, up—, fore—*
supra—	*ofer—, (a)bufan—, up—, geond—*
sur— (additional)	*oðer—, uppan—*
trans—	*geond—, ofer—, ðurh—*
tri—	*ðri—*
twi—	*twi—*
ultra—	*fore—, geond—, for—, ðurh—*
un— (negative)	*un—*
un— (unbind)	*and— (ond—), on—*
uni—	*an—, sam—, anfeald(lic)—*
vice—	*under—*

Suffixing. Old English is as rich in suffixes as in prefixes. In one sense, though, suffixes are more limited—to the formation of various parts of speech: of adjectives, adverbs, nouns, and other adjectives—than prefixes. For although nouns formed through suffixing may be abstract, concrete, particular, or general, etc., and carry definite connotations, their full semantic implication may not be as readily apparent as that of certain prefixes possessing definite functions, such as intensification or negation. Noun-making suffixes in Modern English, such as, *—ness, —ence, —hood, —ment, —ity, —ship,* etc., often carry a variety of special meanings as well as make nouns out of other parts of speech. *Reality, realness, realism,* and *realty,* all derive from the adjective *real,* but with distinctive ranges of meaning. In many cases, further, the same suffix carries different meanings depending upon the stem with which it is combined. Things possess *density*; whereas dense people exhibit *denseness.* Yet stupid people show *stupidity* more than *stupidness.* The same semantic variation holds for *—ish,* and *—ly,* which both form adjectives from nouns, for *mannish* and *manly* are not at all the same quality. In addition, *—ish, —ly,* and *—y,* in forming adjectives, do not fit all words. One might say *doggish* or *doggy,* but not *dogly*—not without a conscious intention to be humorous. In other words, the other words with which suffixes may combine and the meanings of the resultant combinations are, to say the least, highly particular and idiomatic—and in a way logically unpredictable. Of course, there are some "rules." English suffixes *tend* to relate to Latinate suffixes as the English *hearty* to the Latinate *cordial*, that is, they tend to create more personal and vital words than do alternative suffixes from other languages. But there are no hard and fast rules, and the student, again, must in the last analysis depend upon his own word sense.

The result of all this is that a comparative list of Modern and Old English suffixes involves even greater approximation than a similar list of prefixes. Nonetheless, as a guide to the complex semantic changes suffixation has undergone, a complementary comparative list is also provided.

Suffixes by Semantic Class

Adjectival

—*baere*, —*cund*, —*ed(e)*, —*en*, —*erne*, —*faest*, —*feald*, —*ful(l)*, —*ig*, —*iht*, —*isc*, —*leas*, —*lic*, —*maest/*—*mest*, —*od*, —*ol*, —*or*, —*sum*, —*weard*, —*wende*

Adverbial

—*e*, —*lice*, —*maest/*—*mest*, —*unga/*—*inga*

Nominal

Agential

—*bora*, —*end/*—*nd*, —*ere*, —*estre*

Concrete

—*el/*—*ol*, —*els*, —*incel*, —*ing*, —*ling*, —*saete*, —*ware*

Diminutive

—*incel*, —*ing*, —*ling*

Abstract

—*dom*, —*et(t)*, —*had*, —*lac*, —*nes(s)*, —*oð/*—*að*, —*raeden*, —*scipe*, —*stafas*, —*ð(o, u)*, —*u*, —*ung/*—*ing*, —*wist*

Verbal

—*erian/*—*orian*, —*ettan*, —*laecan*, —*nian*, —*(e)sian*

A List of Suffixes

Suffix	Meaning and Function	Use	Examples
—að	See *—oð*		
—baere	Formation of adjectives meaning "productive of, rich in," mostly from nouns	ns	*lustbaere*, agreeable, desirable *tungolbaere*, starry *wigbaere*, warlike
—bora	Formation of masculine agent nouns from other nouns meaning "he who bears or sustains something"	ns	*mundbora*, protector *straelbora*, archer *woðbora*, poet
—cund	Formation of adjectives meaning "like, of the nature of," from nouns and adjectives	ns; a, av	*deofulcund*, diabolical, devilish *gastcund*, spiritual *upcund*, heavenly
—dom[2]	Formation of abstract nouns indicated *state* or *condition*, from other nouns and adjectives	ns; a	*wisdom*, wisdom *swicdom*, treachery *ðeowdom*, service
—e[1]	Formation of adverbs from adjectives	a	*hearde*, hardly, with force *holde*, gently *cwice*, actively
—ed(e)	Formation of adjectives, mostly from nouns, with the meaning "of, made of, equipped with"	ns; +	*faeted*, plated *hringed*, made of rings *hilted*, hilted *hocede*, hooked *sureagede*, blear-eyed
—el, —ol *(—ul)*	Formation of concrete feminine and masculine nouns from other nouns; ; also adjectives from verbal forms	ns; v	*bydel*, messenger *gyrdel*, belt *ðyrel*, hole *stapol*, pillar *beswicol*, deceitful *sprecol*, talkative
—els	Formation of masculine concrete nouns from nouns and other parts of speech	ns; +	*faetels*, vessel *recels*, incense *wrigels*, covering *raedels*, riddle *hydels*, cave, hiding place
—en	Formation of adjectives from nouns (not past participles of strong verbs)	ns	*aettren*, poisonous *gylden*, golden *silfren*, made of silver *aescen*, of ash-wood *hwaeten*, wheaten

Suffix	Meaning and Function	Use	Examples
—end (*—nd*)2	Formation of masculine agent nouns from verbs	v	*agend*, owner *feond*, enemy *metend*, measurer
—ere	Formation of masculine agent nouns mostly from other nouns; later from verbs	ns; v	*fuglere*, fowler *sangere*, singster *baecere*, baker *drincere*, drinker
—erian (*—orian*)	Formation of frequentative and continuative verbs from nouns and adjectives	ns; a	*scimerian*, shimmer *flicorian*, flicker
—erne	Formation of adjectives, for the points of the compass	ns	*suðerne*, southern, etc.
—estre	Formation of agent nouns, first feminine, later masculine, mostly from verbs	v; ns	*miltestre*, harlot *baecestre*, baker *taeppestre*, tavern-keeper
—et(t)	Formation of neuter, abstract nouns, later concrete, commonly from nouns	v; +	*baernet(t)*, burning *rymet*, space *rewet*, rowing *sweofot*, sleeping
—ettan	Formation of intensive or frequentative verbs	v; a, +	*hleapettan*, jump around *laðettan*, loath *onettan*, hasten
—faest	Formation of adjectives from nouns and other adjectives	ns; a	*aerendfaest*, bound on an errand *soðfaest*, righteous *wisfaest*, wise
—feald	Formation of adjectives, especially from numerals	+	*anfeald*, simple, single *drifeald*, threefold
—ful(l)2	Formation of adjectives, especially from abstract nouns, meaning "full of"; some nouns with sense "quantity which fills or would fill"	ns; a	*hyhtful*, hopeful *wuldorful*, wonderful *geornfull*, eager *handful*, handful
—had	Formation of masculine abstract nouns from nouns and adjectives, with idea of state, rank, order, condition, character	ns; a	*geoguð*, time of youth *maegðhad*, virginity *woruldhad*, secular life
—ig1	Formation of adjectives, mainly from nouns	ns	*blodig*, bloody *craeftig*, strong *witig*, knowing, wise

Suffix	Meaning and Function	Use	Examples
—iht	Formation of adjectives from nouns; uncommon	ns	*finiht,* having fins *hocyht,* hooked *ðorniht,* thorny *horniht,* horny
—incel	Formation of neuter diminutives	ns	*cofincel,* little chamber *haeftincel,* slave *husincel,* little house *rapincel,* cord, twine
—ing	Formation of masculine concrete nouns from other nouns and adjectives, meaning "coming from, derived from"; see also —*ung*	ns	*aeðeling,* prince *brenting,* ship *earming,* wretch
—isc	Formation of adjectives from nouns, including names of nations and individuals	ns	*folcisc,* secular *mennisc,* human *Ebrisc,* Hebrew (adj) *Englisc,* English (noun)
—lac	Formation of neuter, abstract nouns from other nouns, indicating motion or action in general	ns	*reaflac,* robbery *wrohtlac,* accusation *witelac,* punishment *saelac,* gift of the sea
—laecan	Formation of verbs from adjectives commonly and nouns	a; ns	*geanlaeccan,* unite *nealaecan,* approach *aefenlaecan,* to become evening
—leas[2]	Formation of adjectives from nouns, with the idea of lacking or being deprived of	ns	*dreamleas,* joyless *cwideleas,* speechless *domleas,* inglorious
—lic[1]	Formation of adjectives normally from nouns or existing adjectives	ns; a	*deofollic,* devilish *munuclic,* monastic *andworuldlic,* worldly
—lice	See —*e*		
—ling	Formation of masculine concrete nouns, from nouns and adjectives; cf. —*ing*	ns; a	*deorling,* favorite *sibbling,* relative *yrðling,* farmer
—maest, —mest	Formation of superlative (locative) adverbs and adjectives (directional)	av; a	*suðmest,* southernmost *niðermest,* undermost *midmest,* in the very center
—nes(s),[1] —nis, —nys	Formation of feminine abstract nouns, especially from adjectives and participial adjectives	a	*beorhtnes,* brightness *sarnes,* pain *ecness,* eternity

Suffix	Meaning and Function	Use	Examples
—nian	Formation of causative and resultative verbs from adjectives and nouns	ns; a	*lacnian*, heal *faestnian*, fasten *ðreatnian*, threaten
—noð	See —oð		
—od	Formation of adjectives; not felt as suffix	+	*forod*, broken, decayed *nacod*, naked
—ol	See —el and —od; also not felt as suffix	+	*sweotol*, plain *deagol*, secret *acol*, timid
—or (—er)	Formation of adjectives; see —od	+	*faeger*, fair *sicor*, sure *snottor*, wise *wacor*, watchful
—oð	Formation of masculine, abstract nouns, from class ii weak verbs	v	*drohtoð*, way of life, experience *langað*, longing *waroð*, shore
—raeden	Formation of abstract feminine nouns from other nouns	ns	*mannraeden*, allegiance *teonraeden*, injury *geferraeden*, companionship
—saete	Formation of masculine names for inhabitants of a place, town, or nation; see —ware	ns	*Sumorsaete*, men of Somerset
—scipe[2]	Formation of abstract masculine nouns from other nouns and adjectives	ns; a	*eorlscipe*, courage *beorscipe*, conviviality *haeðenscipe*, heathenism, paganism
—(e)sian	Formation of verbs usually from nouns and adjectives	ns; a	*maersian*, proclaim *yrsian*, be angry *eg(e)sian*, terrify *bletsian*, bless
—stafas	Formation of abstract masculine nouns, from nouns and adjectives; plural in form	ns; a	*arstafas*, kindness *hearmstafas*, trouble *wyrdstafas*, destiny
—sum	Formation of adjectives, especially from nouns	ns; +	*wynnsum*, delightful *wilsum*, pleasant *angsum*, troublesome *langsum*, enduring
—ð(o), —ð(u)	Formation of feminine abstract nouns, usually from adjectives	a; +	*faehð(o)*, hostility *(ge)treowð*, fidelity *hyhðu*, height *yrmð(u)*, misery *lengð(u)*, length

Suffix	Meaning and Function	Use	Examples
−u (−o)	Formation of feminine abstract nouns from adjectives	a	*menniscu,* humanity, human condition *micelu,* size *wlencu,* pride *haelu,* health *haetu,* heat
−ung[1] *−ing*	Formation of feminine abstract substantives, especially from class ii weak verbs	v	*earnung,* merit *wilnung,* desire *raedung,* lesson
−unga *−inga*	Formation of adverbs from adjectives and some nouns; also intensification	a; ns	*aninga,* entirely *dearnunga,* secretly *eallunga,* entirely *ierrunga,* angrily
−ware	Formation of masculine names for inhabitants of a place, town, or nation; see *−saete*	ns	*burgware,* city-dwellers *Cantware,* men of Kent
−weard	Formation of adjectives from various parts of speech, meaning "toward"	+	*hamweard,* homeward *eastweard,* eastward *ufeweard,* upper *andweard,* present
−wende	Formation of adjectives from existing adjectives and nouns (tendency to be such)	a; ns	*halwende,* healthy *hwilwende,* transitory *leofwende,* amenable
−wist	Formation of abstract feminine nouns, from various parts of speech	+	*huswist,* household *loswist,* loss *neawist,* neighborhood *onwist,* dwelling place *samwist,* living together

A List of Approximate Semantic Correspondences Between Modern and Old English Suffixes

Modern English	Old English
−an, −ian (belonging to or like)	*−cund, −isc; −saete, −ware; −lic*
−ance, −ence (act, fact of)	*−lac, −et(t), −oð, −raeden*
−ancy, −ency (tendency to, state or quality of being)	*−weardnes(s), −wend(e)nes(s); −dom, −had, −nes(s); −raeden, −scipe, −stafas, −ð(o, u), −u*
−ant, −ent (agent)	*−bora, −end, −ere, −estre*
−ard (person, pejorative)	*−ere, −estre; −wiht*

Modern English	Old English
—arian (supportive agent)	—bora; —ere, —estre
—ary (adjective)	—ig, —lic, —etc
—ate (office, function, institution)	—ungnes(s), —lacnes(s); —ambiht, —ðing
—ate (full of)	—ful(l), —cund, —faest, —iht, —sum, —wende
—ate (chemical)	—ed, —en
—ate (verbal)	a— plus causative verb
—ation	—ung, —scaeft, —lac, —nes(s)
—by	—bu, —by
—cy (state or relation of or to privileges)	—had, —nes(s), —wist, —scipe
—dom	—dom
—ed (of, provided with)	—ed
—ed (adjectival)	—ed, —en, —iht
—ee (employee)	—ling
—een (diminutive individual)	—ling
—eer (practicer of profession or activity)	—bora, —end, —ere, —estre
—en	—en
—en (verbal, causative and resultative)	—nian
—er (verbal, frequentative cf. —le)	—erian, —orian; —ol
—er (agent, one connected with)	—ere; —saete, —ware
—erel, —rel	—ere; —el (?)
—ery, —ry	—dom, —lac, —olnes(s); —had; —cund; —stig
—ese	—reord, —tunge, —spraece, —ðeodisc
—esque (having style of)	—baere, —(ol)lic, —(ol)ful(l); —ig, —isc, —lic
—ess	—estre
—et (diminutive)	—incel; —et(t)
—ette (diminutive)	—incel; —ling
—fold	—feald
—ful (careful	—ful(l)
—ful (handfull)	—ful(l)
—hood	—had; —lac; —oð; —lad (way)
—(i)ana (notable sayings, doing of)	—et(t), —lac, —oð
—ic (adjectival)	—ig, —isc, —iht, —en
—ician	—bora, —ere, —estre

Modern English	Old English
—ie, —y (hypocoristic)	—ling; —sige (Wulfsige)
—ify, —fy (make, cause)	a— plus causative verb (cf. perfective prefixes); —ettan; —(e)sian
—ine, —in (adjectival)	—en, —iht, —ig, —lic
—ing (act, fact, practice, material associated with verbal idea, agent, instrument, result, etc.)	—ung/—ing
—ing (personal)	—ing; —ling
—ish	—isc; —lic
—ism (system of doctrinal principles)	—nes(s), —had, —dom; —scipe; —leafa, —lar
—ist (agent, one connected with)	—bora, —ere, —estre; —cund
—ister	—bora, —ere, —estre
—ite	—bora; —saete, —ware; —ere, —estre
—ity	—dom, —had, —nes(s), —scipe, etc.
—ive (characterized by)	—baere, —ig, —lic, —iht, —en, etc.
—ize (transitive and intransitive)	a— plus causative verb —(i)an; —ettan; —(e)sian
—kin, —ikin (endearing, diminutive)	—ling, —ing; —incel
—le (cf. —er verbal)	—lian (cf. twinclian)
—le, —el (nominal)	—el (—ela, —ele)
—less	—leas
—let (diminutive)	—ing, —ling, —incel
—like	—lic
—ling	—ling, —ing
—ly (adjectival)	—lic
—ment	—ung, —lac(nes[s]), —raeden
—mo	—feald, —ð(o, u)
—monger	—mangere
—most	—maest/—mest
—ness	—nes(s)
—ory	—wende, —sum, —weard(lic)
—ous	—baere, —ful(l), —sum; —en
—ship	—scipe
—some	—sum
—ster	—estre; —ere
—th	—ð(o, u)
—ton (cf. —by)	—ere, —ling; —wiht
—ure	—lac, —ung, —nes(s)
—ward, —wards	—weard(es)
—way, —ways	—weg(es)
—wise	—wise
—worthy	—weorð plus —ig
—y	—ig

Compounding. Once more the student is reminded that his own word sense is his best guide to compounding Old English words. The semantic element, that is, the intended meaning, is always most important. Although the structure of compounds in Old (and Modern) English is thoroughly consistent, their actual meanings are often subtle and complex—and unpredictable. Context is paramount!

A compound is the larger word created by combining (usually) two other words. Old English belongs to a group of languages in which the first word (the determinant) usually modifies the second word (the determinatum). There are many exceptions to this, but they tend to involve borrowed structural patterns or special cases, and need not concern the beginning student. Since "compound" verbs are more a matter of affixing than of genuine compounding, the following structural outline is limited to nouns and adjectives. As one can see, the combinative possibilities amount to just about all the "logical" ones.

Patterns of Compounds

Adjectival

1. Adjective plus noun: adjective

   widlast (wide-track) ⟶ "far-wandering"

2. Adjective or adverb plus adjective: adjective

   faestraedlic (firm(ly)-wise) ⟶ "constant"
   eaðgeorn (easily-eager) ⟶ "easily pleased"

3. Adverb plus noun: adjective

   swiðferhð (much/very-spirit) ⟶ "bold, brave"

4. Noun or adjective plus noun: adjective

   beorhtword (bright-word) ⟶ "clear-voiced"
   wulfheort (wolf-hearted) ⟶ "savage"

5. Noun plus adjective: adjective

   limseoc (limb-sick) ⟶ "lame"

Nominal

1. Noun plus noun: noun

   licfaet (body-vessel) ⟶ "body"

2. Adjective plus noun: noun

   yfeladl (evil-sickness) ⟶ "consumption"

3. Adverb plus noun: noun

undercyning (under-king) ⟶ "viceroy"

WORD-ORDER

Word order, like the preceding matters, is both subtle and complex. The following generalizations are offered only as guides to the beginner, who should train himself to look for compositional models in his reading. As a general rule, Old English word-order is more free than that of modern English, yet at the same time it is highly regular and for the most part parallel to modern usage.

The sentence. Every possible combination of subject (S), verb (V), and Object/Complement (O/C) is found in Old English prose and poetry. Most sentences (independent clauses) show the regular modern order: S, V, O/C. When certain adverbs come first (particularly *ne* and *ða*), the order is V, S, O/C. Dependent clauses show many exceptions to these general rules. And as in modern English, artistic and rhetorical emphasis can alter syntactical order, especially in dialogue. When the object is a pronoun, it frequently precedes the main verb.

In dependent clauses (relative, concessive, temporal, conditional, and causal), the normal order is S, O/C, V. Yet many dependent clauses, particularly causal ones, show the regular S, V, O/C order. And as a rule dependent clauses follow the independent clauses on which they depend. Conditional clauses are the primary exception to this pattern.

The parts of speech. The following statements will provide a general guide to the ordering of the parts of speech within sentences.

Demonstratives and *adjectives* normally precede nouns in that order. The word *ealle* and adjectives formed with the suffix −*weard* tend to reverse this order to adjective then demonstrative before nouns. *Ealle* and adjectives formed from −*weard* also follow the nouns they modify. Other exceptions tend to parallel surviving usages such as "trouble enough," "both the big houses," "brothers three," etc. Emphasis again can cause displacement, causing a noun to precede its modifiers. Titles such as king, bishop, etc., generally follow the names they modify. Adjectival genitives usually follow modern patterns, such as "their house," "in John's home," "on the other side of the room," "full of people," etc.

Prepositions usually precede their objects, but may follow them, especially with pronouns. But the postposition is most common when it allows the preposition to precede the main verb, particularly in relative clauses.

Adverbs take a great variety of positions as in modern English. Again, rhetorical and artistic emphasis is the determining factor. In general, however, adverbs precede the items they modify. This is especially true of negatives, which are frequently joined to the words they modify in contracted forms.

The student is again urged to construct sentences upon models from his reading.

R. P. T., Jr.

CONTENTS

Page

PREFACE   v

    Vocabulary selection
    Definitions
    Orthography
    Normalization
    Alphabetization of Entries
    Design of the Dictionary
    Other Features

TABLE OF ABBREVIATIONS   viii

OUTLINE GRAMMAR   ix

WORD-FORMATION AND WORD-ORDER   xiv

    Word-Formation

        Prefixing
        Suffixing
        Compounding

    Word-Order

        The sentence
        The parts of speech

ENGLISH—OLD ENGLISH DICTIONARY   1

OLD ENGLISH—ENGLISH DICTIONARY   91

ENGLISH-OLD ENGLISH DICTIONARY

A

ABANDON   forlaetan 7; laefan i; leosan 2
ABASE   hienan i
ABBOT   abbud (-as) m.
ABJECT   hean
ABODE   bidung (-a) f.
ABOMINABLE   scuniendlic
ABOMINATE   onhyscan i
ABOUT   utan; ymb(e)
ABOVE   ufan(e); uppan; uppe
ABOVE, COMING FROM   ufancund; uppcund
ABOVE, FROM   ufan
ABSTINENCE   forhaefednes f.
ABUNDANCE   wela (-n) m.
ABUSE   niðerian ii; wiergan i
ABYSS   grund (-as) m.; deop (-) n.
ACCESSIBLE   gefere
ACCOMPANY WITH A HARP   sealmian ii
ACCOMPLISH   efnan i; fremman i; raefnan i;
    raefnian ii
ACCORDING TO   aefter; be/bi
ACCOUNT OF, ON   ymb(e)
ACCUSTOM   wennan i
ACCUSTOMED TO, BE   wunian ii
ACHE   acan 6; sargian ii; dolian ii
ACKNOWLEDGE   andettan i
ACQUIRE   begietan 5; -gietan 5; strienan i;
    tilian ii; ðicgan i-5
ACQUISITION   gestreon (-) n.
ACROSS   ofer
ACTION   braegd (-as) m.; daed (-e) f.
ACTIVE   caf; fram; hror; snell; unslaw
ACTIVELY   cafe
ACTRESS   sciernicge (sciernicgan) f.
ADD TO   iecan i
ADORNED   -hread suff.; wraetlic a.
ADVANCE   fyrðran i; steppan i-6; stiepan i
ADVANCEMENT   nyttung (-a) f.
ADVERSARY   andsaca (-n) m.
ADVICE   raed (-as) m.
ADVISE   raedan 7-i
ADZ   adesa (-n) m.
AFAR, FROM   feorran

3

AFFAIR   ðing (-) n.; wise (wisan) f.
AFFLICT   hefigian ii; naetan i; waegan i;
    waelan i
AFFLICTION   hearm (-as) m.
AFRAID   forht; forhtig
AFTER   aefter; hinder; siððan
AFTERWARD   sið
AGAIN   eft; gegn
AGAINST   togegnes; towiðere; wið; wiðere
AGE   ieldu (ielde) f.
AGE, OLD   ieldu (ielde) f.
AGO, LONG   geo/iu
AGREEMENT   gecwidraeden (-a) f.; geðinge (ge-
    ðingu) n.
AGREEMENT, IN   som
AID   fullaest (-as) m.; fylst m. f.
AID   fylstan i
AIR   hwiða (-n) m.; lyft (-a) m. f. n.
ALAS!   eala!
ALE   ealu m. n.
ALERT, BE   warian ii
ALIEN   frem(e)ðe
ALIVE   cwic
ALL   eall
ALLOW   laetan 7; ðolian ii
ALMOST   lytesna; neah av.
ALMS   aelmesse (aelmessan) f.
ALMSGIVING   aelmesse (aelmessan) f.
ALONE   aliepe; ana
ALSO   eac; to
ALTAR   hearg (-as) m.; wiohbed (-) n.
ALTERCATION   geflit (-u) n.
ALTHOUGH   ðeah av. conj.
ALTOGETHER   anunga/aeninga; eall; eallunga
ALWAYS   ealneg; simbel/simble(s); sin- pref.
AMAZE   amasian ii
AMAZED, BE   wafian ii; wundrian ii
AMEN   amen
ANCHOR   ancor (-as) m.
AND   and; oððe
ANEW   niewe; niewinga
ANGEL   engel (englas) m.; gast/gaest (-as) m.
ANGER   anda m.; aebylgð f.; ierrsung (-a) f.;
    torn (-) n.
ANGRILY   ierrunga; wraðe

4

ANGRY   ierre; reðe
ANGRY, BE   belgan 3; ierrsian ii
ANGRY, GROW   belgan 3
ANIMAL   deor (-) n.; neat (-) n.
ANNOUNCE   abeodan 2; bodian ii; meldan i; mel-
     dian ii; secgan i; weman i
ANNOY   dreccan i
ANOINT   smierwan i
ANSWER   andswaru f.
ANSWER   andswarian ii
ANT   aemette (aemettan) f.
ANUS   utgang (-as) m.
ANXIETY   caru (cara) f.
ANXIOUS   carig; enge
ANXIOUS, BE   carian ii
ANXIOUSLY   haedre
ANY   aenig
ANYONE   aeghwa; gehwa; hwa; hwaet
ANYWHERE   aeghwaer; gehwaer
ANYWHERE, FROM   aeghwanan
APART   feorr; sundor
APARTMENT   bur (-as) m.; hof (-u) n.
APERTURE   ðyrel (-u) n.
APPLAUD   flocan 7
APPLE   aeppel (aepplas) m.
APPLE-SHAPED   aeppled
APPLY (SOMETHING TO SOMETHING)   sendan i
APPOINT   teohhian ii
APPORTION   daelan i
APPROACH   gretan i; naegan i; nealaecan i
APPROPRIATE (TO ONESELF)   agnian ii
APPROVAL   gemede n.
ARCH   hwealf (-a) f.
ARID   dryge
ARK   earce f.
ARM   bog (-as) m.; earm (-as) m.
ARM   sierwan i
ARMED   waepned- pref.
ARMED FORCE   fierd (-a) f.; here (hergas) m.
ARMOR   searu (-) n.
ARMY   trum (-) n.
AROUND   ymb(e)
AROUSE   wreccan i
ARRANGE   adihtian ii; racian ii; raedan 7-i;
     redian ii; stihtan i; trymian/trymman i;

5

ARRANGE (CONT.)   witian ii
ARRANGEMENT   stihtung (-a) f.
ARRIVAL   cyme (cymas) m.
ARROGANCE   upahefednes (-a) f.
ARROW   fla (-n) f.; flan (-a) f.; scytel (-as)
    m.; strael (-as, -e) m. f.; straele f.
ARTERY   aeder (aedra) f.; aedre (aedran) f.
ARTIFICE   list (-as) m.
ARTISAN   smið (-as) m.
AS   swa; to
AS SOON AS   siððan
ASCEND   astigan 1; clymmian ii
ASCENDING   staegel
ASCRIBE   gewitan 1
ASHAMED, BE   scamian ii
ASHWOOD   aesc (-as) m.
ASK   ascian ii; biddan i-5; frasian ii; fricgan
    i-5; lengian ii
ASS   assa (-n) m.;eosol (-as) m.
ASSEMBLE   gadrian ii; samnian ii
ASSEMBLY   gemang (-) n.; samnung (-a) f.
ASSENT   tigð (-a) f.
ASSIGN   teohhian ii
ASSIGNED TO   gecnoden
ASTONISHED, BE   wafian ii
ASTONISHMENT   wundrung (-a) f.
AT   aet
AT ALL   wihte
ATHLETE   plegestre f.; plegmann m.
ATONE FOR   betan i
ATONEMENT   bot (-a) f.
ATTACK   anginn n.; -gang (-as) m.; socn (-a) f.;
    storm (-as) m.; ðracu (ðraca) f.
ATTACK, SUDDEN   faer m.; raes (-as) m.
ATTACK   raesan i
ATTEMPT   cunnian ii; fandian ii; fundian ii
ATTEND TO   gieman i; hedan i
ATTRIBUTE   hligan 1
ATTRIBUTED   gecnoden
AVARICE   gitsung (-a) f.; graedignes (-a) f.
AVARICIOUS PERSON   gitsere (gitseras) m.
AVOID   miðan 1
AWAKEN   waecnan i, ii-6
AWARE   cyðig; waer
AWAY   hin- pref.; onweg

AWAY FROM   fram
AWKWARD   aegiepe
AXE   aecs (-a) f.
AXLE   eax f.

B

BACHELOR   hagusteald (-as) m.; hyse (hyssas) m.
BACK   baec (bacu) n.; hrycg (-as) m.
BACK UP   laestan i
BACK   hinder
BACKWARDS   baecling; hinderling; oferbaec
BAD   lysu; lyðre; mah; yfel
BAG   faetels m.; glof (-a) f.
BALD   calu
BALL (MASS, HEAP)   cliewen n.
BAND   heap (-as) m.; scolu f.; teoh (-a) f.;
    weorod (-) n.
BANK, RIVER   ofer (ofras) m.; staeð (staðas) m.
BANNER   cumbol (-) n.; ðuf (-as) m.
BANQUET   dream (-as) m.; symbel (-) n.
BAPTISM   fullwiht m.
BAPTIZE   fulwian ii
BAR   grindel (grindlas) m.; steng (-as) m.
BARE   baer; nacod
BARE, MAKE   berian i
BARGAIN   ceap (-as) m.
BARK   beorcan 3
·BARREN   gaesne
BARROW   hlaw/hlaew (-as) m.; beorg (-as) m.
BASE   grund (-as) m.; truma (-n) m.
BASILISK   basilisca (-n) m.
BATH   baeð (baðu) n.; ðweal (-) n.
BATHE   baðian ii
BATTLE   beadu f.; camp (-as) m.; feoht (-) n.;
    feohte (feohta) f.; guð f.; hild (-a) f.;
    orett (-as) m.; orlege (orelegu) n.; plega
    (-n) m.; tohte (tohtan) f.
BATTLE-STANDARD   cumbol (-) n.; ðuf (-as) m.
BE   beon anv.; wesan anv.
BEACH   faroð (-as) m.; sand (-) n.; waroð (-u) n.
BEAK   nebb (-) n.
BEAR   bera (-n) m.
BEAR   beran 4
BEAR A CHILD   cennan i; strienan i

BEARD   beard (-as) m.
BEARDED   -beard suff.
BEARER   bora (-n) n.
BEAT   beatan 7
BEAUTIFUL   cyrten; gebleod; hiewe; sciene;
    smicre; wlitig
BEAUTIFUL, BECOME   faegerian ii; wlitigian ii
BEAUTY   wlite (-) m.
BECAUSE   for; forhwon
BECOME   weorðan 2
BED   bedd (-) n.; stre(o)wen (streona) f.
BEDECK   bestreðdan i
BEDFELLOW   gebedda (-n) m. f.; gemaecca (-n) m.
BEE   beo (-n) f.
BEER   beor n.
BEETLE   ceafor (-as) m.; wifel m.
BEFIT   dafenian ii
BEFORE   aer prep.; aeror av.; for prep.; foran
    av. prep.
BEFOREHAND   fore
BEGET   cennan i; tieman i
BEGGAR   ðearfa (-n) m.; waedla (-n) n.
BEGGARY   waedl f.
BEGIN   -ginnan 3; niewian ii
BEGINNING   anginn n.; or (-) n.; ord (-) n.
BEGOTTEN   boren
BEGRUDGE, NOT   unnan prp.
BEGUILE   dragan 6; swican 1
BEHAVIOR   gebaere (gebaeru) n.
BEHEAD   beheafdian ii
BEHIND   onlast(e)
BEHIND, FROM   hindan
BEING   wiht (-a, -e) f. n.
BELCH   bealcettan i; bealcian ii; bielcan i;
    rocettan i
BELIEF   geleafa (-n) m.
BELIEVE   liefan i; treowan i
BELLY   hrif (-u) n.; wamb (-a) f.
BELONGING TO   -lang suff.
BELOVED   leof; swaes
BELOW   niðer; niðan(e)
BELOW, FROM   niðan(e)
BELT   fetel (-as) m.; gyrdels (-as) m.
BENCH   benc (-a) f.
BEND   biegan i; bugan 2; wraestan i

BEND LOW   hnigan 1
BENEFIT   ar (-a) f.; hroðor (hroðras) m.
BEREAVE   astiepan i; reofan 2
BESET   swingan 3
BESIDE   be/bi av. pref. prep. post pos.
BEST   betst; selest
BESTOW   tigðian ii
BESTREW   bestreddan i
BETOKEN   beacnian ii; tacnian ii
BETTER   bet av.; betera a.; sel av.; selra a.
BETTER, GROW   batian ii
BETWEEN   betweon; betweonum; betweox
BEWAIL   cwiðan i; rarian ii
BEYOND   geond; uton
BIER   baer (-a) f.
BIG   micel
BILL (OF A BIRD)   nebb (-) n.
BILLOW   waðuma (-n) m.
BILLOW   yðrian ii
BIND   bindan 3; cyppan i; tiegan i
BINDER   bindere (binderas) m.
BIRD   bridd (-as) m.; fugol (fuglas) m.
BIRTH   byrd (-a) f.; byrdu f.
BISHOP   biscop (-as) m.
BIT   stycce (styccu) n.
BITE   slite m.
BITE   baetan i; bitan 1
BITTER   afor; sticol
BLACK   blaec; sweart; wann
BLACK, DULL   blaec
BLACKENED   salwed
BLAME   edwit (-) n.
BLAME   gewitan 1; taelan i; ðrafian ii
BLAMELESS   unscaeðig; untaele
BLAST   blaest (-as) m.; fnaest m.
BLEACH   blaecan i
BLEAT   blaetan i
BLEED   bledan i; swaetan i
BLESS   bletsian ii; segnian ii
BLESSED   eadig
BLESSING   bletsung (-a) f.; segnung (-a) f.
BLIND   blendan i
BLIND   blind
BLISS   wynn (-a) f.
BLISTER   blegen f.

BLOOD   blod (-) n.; dreor m.; heolfor n.; swat m.
BLOODY   blodig; dreorig; heolfrig; swatig
BLOODY, MAKE   blodigian ii
BLOOM   blostm (-as) m.; blostma (-n) m.
BLOOM   blowan 7; rogian ii
BLOT   splott (-as) m.
BLOT OUT   adilegian ii
BLOW   drepe (drepas) m.; dynt (-as) m.; geslieht (-as) m.; slege (slegas) m.; sweng (-as) m.
BLOW   blawan 7; wawan 7
BLOWING   blaest (-as) m.
BLUE   haewen
BLUE-GREEN-GRAY   haewen
BLUE-PURPLE   haewen
BLUNT   biegan i
BOAR   eofor (-as) m.
BOARD   bord (-) n.
BOAST   gielp m. n.
BOAST   gielpan 3
BOAT   bat (-as) m.
BODY   lic (-) n.
BOIL   seoðan 2
BOLD   arod; beald; caf; cene; deor; fram; modig; rof; snell; ðrist; ðyhtig
BOLD, BE   bealdian ii
BOLD, MAKE   hierdan i
BOLDLY   ðriste
BOLDNESS   bieldu (-) f.; cenðu (cenða) f.
BOLT   clustor (clustru) n.; grindel (grindlas) m.; loc (-u) n.; loca (-n) m.; scyttels (-) m.; steng (-as) m.
BOND   bend (-as, -a) m. f.; bind (-) n.; fetera f. pl.; haeft (-as) m.; wrasen (wrasna) f.; wriða (-n) m.
BONE   ban (-) n.
BOOK   boc (bec) f.
BOOTY   huð (-a) f.; reaf (-) n.
BOOTY, TAKE   hyðan i
BORDER   fnaed (fnadu) n.; rand (-as) m.
BORN   boren
BORN, BE   waecnan i, ii-6
BOSOM   bosm (-as) m.; faeðm (-as) m.
BOTH   aeghwaeðer; begen
BOTHER ABOUT   hedan i; murnan 3
BOTTLE, LEATHER   cyll (-a) f.

BOTTOM   botm m.; flor (-as) m.; grund (-as) m.
BOTTOMLESS   grundleas; ungrynde
BOUNDARY   gemaere (gemaeru) n.; mearc (-as) m.
BOW (WEAPON)   boga (-n) m.
BOW OF A SHIP   stefn (-as) m.; stefna (-n) m.
BOW DOWN   hnaegan i; hnigan 1; lutan 2
BOW THE HEAD   hnipian ii
BOWMAN   sceotend (-as) m.
BRAMBLE   braemel (-as) m.; fyrs (-as) m.
BRANCH   bog (-as) m.; stofn m. f.
BRANCH OUT   telgian ii
BRANDISHING   braegd (-as) m.
BRAVE   beald; fram; heard
BREADTH   braedu f.
BREAK   brecan 5/4; breotan 2; fretan 5; scaenan i
BREAK UP   bryttian ii
BREAKING   brec (-) n.
BREAST   breost (-) n.; hreðer (-as) m.; sefa (-n)
    m.
BREATH   aeðm (-as) m.; fnaest m.; oroð n.
BREEZE   hwiða (-n) m.
BRIDE   bryd (-e) f.
BRIDEGROOM   brydguma (-n) m.
BRIDGE   brycg (-a) f.
BRIDGE   brycgan i; brycgian ii
BRIDLE   brigdels (-as) m.
BRIDLE   baetan i
BRIGHT   beorht; blac; brun; scir; torht
BRIGHTEN   bierhtan i
BRIGHTLY   swegle
BRIGHTNESS   bierhtu (-) f.; breahtm (-as) m.
BRILLIANT, MAKE   scaenan i
BRING   beran 4; bringan i
BROAD   brad; sid
BROKEN CONDITION   brecða (-n) m.
BROOD OVER   seoðan 2
BROOK   broc (-as) m.; burna (-n) m.; burne (bur-
    nan) f.
BROTHER   broðor (-, broðru) m.
BROW   braew (-as) m.
BROWN, DULL   brunwan(n); dunn
BROWN, GLOSSY   brun
BRUISE   laela (-n) m.
BUCKLE   gespang n.; gespann n.; spang (-e) f.
BUFFOON   sceawend (-as) m.

11

BUILD   raeran i; timbran i; timbrian ii
BUILDER   bylda (-n) m.
BUILDING   aern (-) n.; bold (-) n.; hus (-) n.;
    traef (trafu) n.
BUILDING MATERIAL   timber (-) n.
BULK   micelnes (-a) f.
BURDEN   hlaest (-) n.
BURIAL MOUND   hlaw/hlaew (-as) m.; beorg (-as) m.
BURN   baernan i; biernan 3; swaelan i; swelan 4;
    tinnan 3
BURN UP   aelan i
BURNING   aelung (-a) f.; byrne m.
BURNING   fyren
BURNING WOOD   brand (-as) m.
BURST   berstan 3
BURIER   byrgend (-as) m.
BURY   byrgan i
BUSHEL   byden (-a) f.; bydenfaet (bydenfatu) n.
BUSINESS   bisigu (bisiga) f.; ðing (-) n.
BUSINESS TRANSACTION   ceap (-as) m.; ceapung (-a)
    f.
BUSINESS, DO   ceapian ii; ciepan i; ðingian ii
BUSY   bisig
BUT   ac; butan
BUTTER   cubutere f.
BUY   bycgan i; ceapian ii
BYRNIE   byrne (byrnan) f.; sierce (siercan) f.

C

CAJOLERY   olaecung (-a) f.
CALAMITY   hryre m.; ðrea (-) m. f. n.
CALF   cealf (-ru) m.; stierc (-) n.
CALL   ceallian ii; ciegan i; cleopian ii; hatan 7
CALLED, BE   hatan 7
CALL OUT   ciegan i; cierman i; clipian ii
CAN   magan prp.
CANDLE   candel (-a) f.
CANON   regol (-as) m.
CANOPY   baelc (-as) m.
CANTICLE   cantic (-as) m.; organ (-as) m.
CAPTIVE   haeft (-as) m.; wealh (wealas) m.
CAPTURE   haeftan i
CARE   caru (cara) f.; giemen (-a) f.
CARE   reccan i

12

CARE ABOUT   gieman i; murnan 3; sinnan 3
CARELESSNESS   recceliest f.
CARGO   fearm (-as) m.; hlaest (-) n.
CARNAGE   wael (walu) n.
CAROUSE   symblian ii
CARRIER   bora (-n) n.
CARRION   aes n.
CARRY   beran 4; wegan 5
CARRY OUT   diegan i; hiegan i; laestan i
CART   craet (cratu) n.; waegn (-as) m.
CAT   catt (-as) m.; catte (cattan) f.
CATTLE   neat (-) n.; orf (-) n.; weorf (-) n.
CAUSE   intinga (-n) m.
CAUSE   laetan 7
CAUTIOUS   waer
CAVE   scraef (scrafu) n.
CEASE   blinnan 3; swaðrian/sweðrian ii
CEDAR   ceder m. f. n.
CEILING   first (-a) f.
CELESTIAL   heofoncund; ufancund; uppcund; upplic
CELT   wealh (wealas) m.
CERTAIN   cuð; gewiss; witod
CERTAINLY   witodlice
CHAFFER   ceafor (-as) m.; wifel m.
CHAIN   lann (-a) f.; racente (racentan) f. sima
     (-n) m.; teag (-a) f.
CHAIN   clemman i
CHAIR   stol (-as) m.
CHALICE   calic (-as) m.
CHANCE   neðan i
CHANGE   gewrixle (gewrixlu) n.; wendung (-a) f.;
     wierp m.
CHANGE OF COLOR   brigd (-) n.
CHANGE   fagian ii; wrixlan i
CHANT   cantic (-as) m.; organ (-as) m.
CHAOS   dwolma m.
CHAPEL   gebedhus (-) n.
CHARIOT   scrid (-u) n.
CHARM, MAGICAL   malscrung (-a) f.
CHASTE   cusc
CHEAT   blencan i; searwian ii
CHEEK   hleor (-) n.
CHEER   retan i; taetan i
CHEERFUL   rot
CHEF   coc (-as) m.

CHERUBIM   cherubin
CHEST (BODY)   breost (-) n.
CHEST (STORAGE)   earc (-a) m. f.; earce f.
CHEW   ceowan 2
CHIEF   fruma (-n) m.
CHIEFTAN   bealdor m.; strengel (strenglas) m.
CHILD   bearn (-) m.; umbor (-) n.
CHILDHOOD   cildhad (-as) m.
CHILDISH   cildisc
CHILL   ciele m.
CHOICE   cyre (-) m.
CHOICE   cystig
CHOICEST   cyst (-e) f.
CHOOSE   ceosan 2
CHRISTIAN   cristen
CHURCH   cirice (cirican) f.
CHURL   ceorl (-as) m.
CIRCLE   circul (-as) m.
CIRCLE   hwierfan i; windan 3
CIRCUIT   hwearft (-as) m.; hwyrft (-as) m.
CITY   ceaster (ceastra) f.
CLAN   maegð (-a) f.
CLANSHIP   sibb (-a) f.
CLAP   flocan 7
CLASH   gehast/gehnaest n.; mitting f.
CLASH   hnitan 1
CLASP   gespang n.; gespann n.; spang (-e) f.
CLAW   clawu (clawa) f.; clea (-n) f.
CLAY   lam n.
CLAY, OF   laemen
CLEAN   feormian ii; hlutrian i
CLEAN   claene
CLEANER   feormend (-) m.
CLEANSE   claensian ii; faelsian ii
CLEAR   ryman i
CLEAR, MAKE   sciran i; sweotolian ii
CLEAR THE THROAT   cohhettan i
CLEAR   cuð; hador; hlutor; scir; sweotol
CLEARLY   cuðe; leohte; swegle
CLEAVE   cleofan 2
CLEVER   gleaw
CLIFF   clif (-u) n.; hlið (-, -u) n.; weall (-as)
    m.
CLIMB   astigan 1; clymmian ii
CLINGING   clibbor

14

CLOAK   rift(e) n.
CLOSE   clysan i; dyttan i; hlidan 1; lucan 2
CLOSE TOGETHER   geneahsen
CLOSELY   nearwe
CLOSET   cofa (-n) m.
CLOTH   clað (-as) m.; webb (-u) n.
CLOTHE   scierpan i
CLOTHED   hread
CLOTHES   clað (-as) m.
CLOTHING   rift(e) n.; sceorp (-) m.; scierpla
    (-n) m.
CLOUD   sceo m.; wolcen (wolcnas, wolcu) m. n.
CLUB   sagol (-as) m.
COAL   col (-u) n.
COAL, GLOWING   gled (-a) f.
COAT   ham(a) (-as, -n) m.
COATED   ham
COCK-CROW   hancraed m.
COHABITATION   gemacnes f.; gemacscipe m.; haemed
    n.; wifcyððu f.
COHABIT WITH   haeman i
COIN   scaett (-as) m.
COITION   haemed m.
COLD   ceald
COLLECT   gadrian ii
COLOR   bleo (-) n.; hiew (-) n.; tielg (-as) m.
COLORED   fag; hiewe
COMBAT   wig (-) n.
COMBINE   mengan i
COME   cuman 4; gan anv.
COME ASHORE   lendan i
COMEDIENNE   sciernicge (sciernicgan) f.
COMER   cuma (-n) m.
COMET   cometa (-n) m.
COMFORT   ellnian ii; frefran i; miltsian ii
COMING   cyme (cymas) m.
COMING FROM   -cund suff.
COMITATUS   folgað (-as) m.
COMMAND   bann (-) n.; bebod (-) n.; gebod (-) n.;
    haes (-e) f.
COMMAND   beodan 2
COMMANDMENT   bebod (-) n.; gebod (-) n.
COMMENTATOR   trahtere (trahteras) m.
COMMIT A CRIME   firenian ii
COMMIT TO SOMEONE   taecan i

15

COMMON   gemaene
COMMON, SHARED IN   gemaene
COMMOTION   geðring n.; ðreat (-as) m.
COMMUNITY   gemana (-n) m.
COMPANION   gaedeling (-as) m.; gefara (-n) m.;
     gehlaeða (-n) m.; gemaecca (-n) m.; gesið
     (-as) m.; handgesella (-n) m.; selda (-n)
     m.; stealla (-n) m.
COMPANY   gad/gaed n.; hos f.; teoh (-a) f.
COMPARISON   wiðmetennes (-a) f.
COMPEL   baedan i; niedan i; ðrafian ii
COMPETE   flitan 1
COMPLETE   fullian ii
COMPLETELY   anunga/aeninga; aeghwaes
COMPULSION (LEVY)   bad f.
COMRADE   gefara (-n) m.
CONCEAL   beorgan 3; diernan i; helan 4; miðan 1
CONCEALED   deagol/deogol; dierne; onhaele
CONCEALING   heoloð- pref.
CONCEIT   upahefednes (-a) f.
CONCEPTION   eacnung (-a) f.
CONCERNING   fram prep.
CONCILIATE   seman i; ðingian ii
CONCILIATION   frið (-as, -u) m. n.; sibb (-a) f.
CONDITION   had (-as) m.
CONDITION (STIPULATION)   araednes (-a) f.
CONDUCT ONESELF   drohtian ii; gebaeran i
CONFESS   andettan i
CONFINE   heaðorian ii; nearwian ii; nierwan i
CONFINED   enge; nearu
CONFINEMENT   engu (enge) f.
CONFIRM   staðolian ii
CONFIRMATION   trumnað m.
CONFLICT   mitting f.
CONFUSION   dwolma m.
CONJUGAL   gemaclic
CONSCIOUS   waer; wittig
CONSCIOUSNESS   gemynd (-e, -) f. n.; witt n.
CONSECRATE   bledsian/bletsian ii
CONSEQUENCE   finta (-n) m.
CONSIDER   smeagan i; trahtian ii
CONSIDERATE   ðancol
CONSIDERATION   ðeahtung (-a) f.
CONSOLATION   frofor (frofra) f.
CONSOLE   frefran i

CONSORT   gebedda (-n) m. f.
CONSTRAIN   ðraestan i
CONSTRAINT   bind (-) n.
CONSUME   gedrettan i; ðecgan i
CONSUMING   -aeta suff.
CONTACT WITH, IN   getenge
CONTAINER   faet (fatu) n.
CONTEMPT   forhogodnes f.
CONTEND   flitan 1
CONTENTIOUSNESS   ðraeft (-) n.
CONTEST   fitt (-) n.; geflit (-u) n.
CONTINUAL   singal
CONTINUALLY   singala; singales
CONTINUOUS   gadortang; sin- pref.
CONTRIVED WITH CUNNING   searu- pref.
CONTROL   weald f. n.; wield (-) n.
CONTROL   stefnan i; wealdan 7
CONVERSATION   spellung (-a) f.; spraec (-a) f.
CONVERT   cierran i
COOK   coc (-as) m.
COOK   seoðan 2
COOKING PAN   cocerpanne (-) f.
COOL   col; wlacu
COOL OFF   colian ii; caelan i
COOLNESS   ciele m.
COPPER   ar n.
CORD   sada (-n) m.; teag (-a) f.
CORN   hwaete m.
CORNER   hwam (-as) m.; sceat (-as) m.
CORPSE   hraw/hraew (-) n.; lic (-) n.: ne(o)
    (neas) m.; wael (walu) n.
CORRODE   etan 5
CORRUPTION   brosnung (-a) f.; mierrelse f.
CORSLET   byrne (byrnan) f.; sierce (siercan) f.
COUCH   leger (-u) n.
COUGH   cohhettan i
COUNCIL   maeðel (-u) n.; ðeaht (-u) f. n.; ðeah-
    tung (-a) f.
COUNCILLOR   wita (-n) m.
COUNSEL   lar (-a) f.
COUNT   rim (-) n.
COUNT   riman i; tellan i
COUNTENANCE   andwlita (-n) m.; wlite (-) m.
COUNTRY   eðel (eðlas) m.; land (-) n.
COUNTRY, OPEN   feld (-as) m.

17

COURAGE   mod (-as) m.
COURSE   -gang (-as) m.; lad (-a, -) f. n.; spor
     n.
COURT   hof (-u) n.
COURT-YARD   geard (-as) m.; hof (-u) n.
COUSIN   suhterga m.
COVER   helan 4; hlidan 1; hwealfan i; ðeccan i;
     wreon i
COVER WITH A HELMET   helman/hylman i; helmian ii
COVERING   bere (beran) f.; baelc (-as) m.; hama
     (-n) m.; hlid (-u) n.; hreoða (-n) m.; hrof
     (-as) m.; wrigels (-) n.
COVET   gitsian ii
COW   cu (cy, cye) f.
COWL   bolla (-n) m.
CRACKLE   brastlian ii
CRACKLING   brastl m.
CRAFTSMAN   wyrhta (-n) m.
CRAG   torr (-as) m.
CRAWL   slincan 3
CREATE   scieppan i-6
CREATION   frumð/frymð (-as) m.; gescaeft (-a) f.
CREATOR   meotod m.; scieppend m.
CREATURE   wiht (-a, -e) f. n.
CREEP   creopan 2; snican 1
CRIME   faehð (-a) f.; firen (-a) f.; man (-) n.;
     wamm (-as, -) m. n.
CRIMINAL   wearg (-as) m.
CROOKED   woh; wrang
CROSS   beam (-as) m.; gealga (-n) m.; rod (-a) f.
CROSSWISE   ðweorh
CROWD   draeg n.; geðrang (-) n.; heap (-as) m.;
     hwearf (-as) m.
CROWD   crudan 2; ðringan 3; ðryccan i
CRUEL   fell; gram; reow; sliðe(n); stierne; wyl-
     fen
CRUELLY   bitere
CRUMBLE   dreosan 2; worian ii
CRUSH   brysan i
CRUST   rind (-a) f.
CRY   cierm (-as) m.; hream (-as) m.
CRY ALOUD   styrman i
CRY OUT   cierman i; cleopian ii; graedan i; hro-
     pan 7
CRYSTAL   cristalla (-n) m.

CUB   hwelp (-as) m.
CUCKOO   geac (-as) m.
CUNNING   list (-as) m.
CUP   bolla (-n) m.; faet (fatu) n.; orc (-as)m.;
    scenc (-a) f.
CUPBEARER   byrele (byrelas) m.
CURE   lacnian ii
CURIOSITY   fyrwitt n.
CURRENT   stream (-as) m.
CURSE   wiergðu (wiergða) f.
CURSE   wiergan i
CURVED   geap
CUSHION   bolster (bolstras) m.
CUSTODY   geheald n.; haeft (-as) m.; heord (-a)
    f.; waru (wara) f.
CUSTOM   ðeaw (-as) m.; wuna (-n) m.
CUSTOMARY   genge; gewunelic
CUT   bite (-) m.; slite m.; snaed (-as) m.
CUT   bitan 1; ceorfan 3; scieran 4; slitan 1;
    snaedan i; sniðan 1; ðwitan 1
CUT DOWN   heawan 7
CUT THE HAIR OF   efsian ii
CUT OFF   scieran 4
CUT OFF FROM   sceard
CUTTING   biter
CYST   wenn (-as, -a) m. f.

D

DAILY   daeghwaemlice
DALE   dael (dalu) n.
DAMAGE   byrst (-as) m.
DAMAGE   mierran i; scierdan i
DANGER   faer m.
DANGEROUS   fraecne; sliðe(n)
DARE   durran prp.
DARING   neðung (-a) f.; noð (-a) f.
DARING   dyrstig; ðrist
DARINGLY   ðriste
DARK   blaec; deagol/deogol; deorc; dimm; earp;
    fealu; hasu; mierce; nifol; salwig-; salu;
    sweart; ðeostor; wann
DARK, GROW   drysmian ii; fealwian ii; nipan 1;
    solian ii; swamian ii; sweorcan 3; ðeostrian
    ii; wanian ii

19

DARKENED   salwed
DARKNESS   genip (-u) n.; hoðma (-n) m.; mierce
     n.; ðeostru f.
DART   daroð (-as) m.; pil (-as) m.
DAWN   daegraed (-) n.; uht- pref.; uhta (-n) m.
DAWN   dagian ii
DAY   daeg (dagas) m.; dogor (-) m. n.; mergen/
     morgen (morgnas)m.; niht f.
DAYBREAK   aering f.
DEAD   belifd; dead
DEAF   deaf
DEALINGS   gemana (-n) m.
DEAR   diere; leof; swaes
DEAR ONE   dierling (-as) m.
DEATH   bana (-n) m.; cwalu f.; cwealm (-as) m.;
     cwield m. f. n.; deað (-as) m.; fiell (-as)
     m.; hryre m.; swylt (-as) m.
DEATH, PUT TO   cwellan i; swebban i
DEATH, SLEEP IN   swefan 5
DECADE   hund- pref.
DECAY   brosnung (-a) f.
DECAY   brosnian ii
DECEIT   facen (-) n.; leasung (-a) f.; lot (-u)
     n.; swic (-u) n.
DECEITFUL   faecne; flah; swice; swicol
DECEIVE   blencan i; blendan i; swican 1
DECORATE   gierwan i; hyrstan i
DECREE   scrifan 1
DECREPIT   forworen
DEED   daed (-e) f.
DEEP   deop
DEEPLY   deope
DEFEND   ealgian ii; werian i
DEFENDER   gehola (-n) m.
DEFENSE   beorg (-as) m.
DEFER   ieldan i
DEFILE   fylan i; wemman i; widlian ii
DELAY   bid n.; ieldung (-a) f.
DELAY   gaelan i; ieldan i; lengan i
DELIBERATE   eahtian ii; ðridian ii
DELIBERATION   eahtung (-a) f.
DEN   denn (-) n.
DEPART   feorrsian ii; leoran i,ii-2; scacan 6;
     swician ii; witan 1
DEPENDENT ON   -lang suff.

DEPRIVE OF   bedaelan i; naeman i; twaefan i
DEPRIVED OF   sceard
DERISION   bismer m. f. n.; hlaeg n.
DESCEND   stigan 1
DESCENDANT   maga (-n) m.; team m.
DESERT   earnung (-a) f.; waesten (-as, -u) m. n.;
    wyrht (-a, -) f. n.
DESIRABLE   willsum
DESIRE   lust (-as) m.
DESIRE   friclan i; gitsian ii; lystan i
DESIRED   willsum
DESIROUS   frynidig; georn
DESIROUSLY   georne
DESOLATE   weste
DESPAIRING   orwene
DESPISE   aewan i; bismerian ii; wiergan i
DESPOIL   hloðian ii
DESTINE   witian ii
DESTINY   gescaeft (-a) f.; wyrd (-e) f.
DESTINED TO, BE   sculan prp.
DESTITUTE   gaesne; orhlytte; waedle
DESTITUTION   waedl f.
DESTROY   cinnan 3; scierdan i; spildan i; wier-
    dan i
DESTRUCTION   cwield m. f. n.
DETACH   aliðian ii
DETERMINE   tengan i
DEVASTATE   ieðan i; westan i
DEVICE   searu (-) n.
DEVIL   deofol (deoflas) m.
DEVOUR   fretan 5; swelgan 3
DEW   deaw m.
DEWY   deawig; urig- pref.
DICE, GAME OF   taefl (-a) f. n.
DIE, GAMING   taefl (-a) f. n.; teosal (-as) m.
DIE   cwelan 4; faran 6; gewitan 1; leoran i, ii-
    2; sweltan 3
DIE OUT   swaðrian/sweðrian ii
DIFFICULT   earfoðlic
DIFFICULTY   earfoð (-u) n.; nearu (nearwa) f.
DIG   delfan 3; grafan 6
DIGNITY   ðyncðo (ðyncða) f.
DIM   dimmian ii
DIM   dimm
DIMINISH   minsian ii

DIN   dyne m. n.
DIN, MAKE A   dynian i
DIP   diefan i; dyppan i
DIRECT   stieran i; taecan i; wisian ii
DIRECTIONS, IN ALL   aeghwider
DIRELY   sliđe
DIRT   adela (-n) m.; gor (-u) n.; meox n.;
    scearn n.
DIRTY   sol
DIRTY PLACE   adela (-n) m.
DISAPPEAR   dwinan 1; swađrian/sweđrian ii
DISCIPLE   geongra (-n) m.; leornungcniht (-as) m.
DISCIPLESHIP   geongordom m.; geongorsciepe m.
DISCOURSE   mađelian ii; maeđlan i; maelan i;
    spellian ii
DISCRIMINATING   scadwis; scearp
DISFAVOR   aefest (-e) f.
DISGRACE   aewisc f. n.; scand (-a) f.
DISH   disc (-as) m.
DISINTEGRATE   brosnian ii; dreosan 2; meltan 3;
    molsnian ii
DISLIKE   aefest (-e) f.
DISPENSER   brytta (-n) m.
DISPERSE   stencan i; swengan i
DISPLEASE   đreotan 2
DISPLEASURE   aefđanca m.
DISPOSITION   mod (-as) m.
DISSIMULATE   miđan 1; searwian ii
DISSOLVE   meltan 3
DISTINCTION   weorđung (-a) f.
DISTINGUISH BETWEEN   scadan 7
DISTINGUISHED   weorđ
DISTRESS   caru (cara) f.; nearu (nearwa) f.;
    đrea m. f. n.; wa (-n) m.
DISTRESS, SUFFER   carian ii
DISTRESSED   seoslig
DISTRIBUTE   bryttian ii
DISTRIBUTION   dal (-) n.; gedal (-) n.
DISTRIBUTOR   brytta (-n) m.
DISTURB   drefan i; gemarian ii; strudan 2; sty-
    rian i
DIVE   dufan 2
DIVIDE   brytnian ii; daelan i; scadan 7
DIVINE   heofonlic
DO   don anv.; dreogan 2; fremman i

DO AWAY WITH   forþyndan i
DOCTOR   laece (laecas) m.
DOCUMENT, WRITTEN   writ (-u) n.
DOE   hind (-a) f.
DOG   hund (-as) m.
DONKEY   eosol (-as) m.
DOOM   dom (-as) m.
DOOMED   faege
DOOR   duru (dura) f.
DOUBT   tweo (-n) m.
DOUBT   tweo(ga)n ii
DOUGHTY   dyhtig; ðyhtig
DOVE   culfer/culfre (culfran) f.
DOWN   niðer; ofdune
DOWNFALL   gecring (-as) m.; hryre m.
DOWNWARDLY TURNED   niðerheald; niðerweard
DOZE   hnappian ii
DRAGON   draca (-n) m.; wyrm (-as) m.
DRAW   teon 2; togian ii
DRAW A SWORD   bregdan 3
DREAD   draedan 7
DREADFUL   unhiere
DREAM   swefn (-) n.
DREAM   maetan i; swefnian ii
DREARY   dreorig
DRINK   drinc/drync (-as) m.
DRINK   drencan i; drincan 3
DRIP   dreopian ii; dropettan i
DRIPPING   dropung (-a) f.
DRIVE   drifan 1; wrecan 5
DRIVE AWAY   draefan i
DRIVE ON   drifan 1
DROOP   drusian ii; sanian ii
DROP   dropa (-n) m.
DROP   dropettan i
DROPPING   dreorung (-a) f.
DROSS   sinder n. pl.
DROWN   drencan i
DRUG   pigment ?
DRUNKENNESS   druncennes f.
DRY   drygan i; ðyrran i
DRY, BECOME   drugian ii
DRY UP   drygan i; forwisnian ii; spiercan i
DRY   dryge; ðyrre
DULL   medwis

23

DUMB   dumb
DUNG   meox n.; scearn n.; tord (-) n.
DUSKY   hasu; salu
DUST   dust n.; molde (moldan) f.
DWARF   dweorg (-as) m.
DWELL   buan 7/iii; eardian ii; wunian ii
DWELLERS IN   -waran;-waras; -ware; -waru pl.
    suff.
DWELLING   haga (-n) m.; ham (-as) m.; sele (-)
    m.; salor (-) m.; steald (-) n.
DWELLING PLACE   wic (-) n.; wunung (-a) f.
DYE   tielg (-as) m.
DYE, BLUE   wad m.

E

EACH   aelc; aeghwilc; hwilc
EACH ONE   gehwa
EAGER   georn
EAGER FOR   fus
EAGERLY   georne
EAR   eare (earan) n.
EARL   eorl (-as) m.
EARLY   aern
EARN   earnian ii
EARNESTNESS   eornost (-a) f.
EARTH   eorðe (eorðan) f.; folde (foldan) f.;
    molde (moldan) f.
EARTH (MATERIAL)   hruse (hrusan) f.
EARTHEN   laemen
EARTHENWARE   lam n.
EASILY   eað; eaðe
EAST   east
EAST, FROM THE   eastan
EASTERN   easterne; easteweard
EASY   eaðe
EAT   biergan i; etan 5; fretan 5; mesan i
EATER   -aeta suff.
EATING   aet m. f.
EBB   ebbian ii
EBB-TIDE   ebba m.
EDGE   breord (-as) m.; brim (-u) n.; ecg (-a) f.;
    laerig (-) m.
EEL   ael (-as) m.
EERIE   unhiere

EIGHT   eahta
EIGHTH   eahta
EIGHTEENTH   eahtteoða
EITHER   aeghwaeðer
EITHER . . . OR   ge . . . ge
EFFECT   wyrcan i
EFFORT   gewinn (-) n.
EGG   aeg (-ru) n.
ELECT   ceosan 2
ELEGANT   hnesclic; riclic; smicre; swancor
ELEPHANT   elpend (-) m.
ELEVATE   raeran i; stiepan i
ELEVATED   steap
ELEVATED SURFACE   hrycg (-as) m.
ELEVEN   endleofan
ELF   aelf (ielfe, ylfe) m. f.
ELITE   aeðelu f. n. pl.; cyst (-e) f.
ELOQUENT   cwedol; getynge
ELSE   elles
ELSEWHERE   elleshwergen; ellor
ELSEWHERE, FROM   el(e)- pref.
EMBARRASSMENT   scamu (scama) f.
EMBER   col (-u) n.
EMBER, GLOWING   gled (-a) f.
EMBOLDEN   bieldan i
EMBOSSED   aeppled
EMBRACE   faeðm (-as) m.
EMBRACE   clyppan i; faeðman i; faeðmian ii
EMPEROR   casere (caseras) m.
EMPTY   aemettig; idelc; ieðe; tom
EMPTY, BECOME   idlian ii
EMULATE   ellnian ii; laestan i
ENCAMP   wician ii
ENCHANTMENT   gealdor (gealdru) n.
ENCLOSE   forðylman i; tynan i
ENCLOSED PLACE   cofa (-n) m.; tun (-as) m.
ENCLOSURE   clus (-a) f.; codor (-as) m.; geard
    (-as) m.; haga (-n) m.
ENCOUNTER   metung (-a) f.
ENCOUNTER   metan i
ENCOURAGE   bieldan i; hiertan i
END   ende (endas) m.
END   endian ii
ENDURE   diegan i; ðrowian ii
ENEMY   feond (-as, fiend) m.; hettend (-) m.

25

ENFOLD   waefan i
ENGRAVE   grafan 6
ENJOY   brucan 2; neotan 2; nyttian ii
ENNOBLE   aeðelian ii
ENOUGH   geneahhe; neah
ENRAGE   gremian ii
ENSIGN   cumbol (-) n.; segn (-as, -) m. n.
ENTERPRISE   sið (-as) m.
ENTERTAIN   feormian ii; giestliðian ii
ENTICE   weman i
ENTIRELY   ealles; eallunga
ENTRANCE   muð (-as) m.; muða (-n) m.
ENTREAT   bensian ii; giernan i
ENUMERATE   rimian i
ENUMERATION   rim (-) n.
ENVIOUS   aefestig
EQUALIZE   efenettan i
EQUAL TO   gelic
EQUALLY   endemes(t)
EQUIP   geatwan i; hyrstan i; sierwan i
EQUIPMENT   geatwe f. pl.; hyrst (-) f.
EQUIPPED SPLENDIDLY   geatolic
ERASE   adilegian ii
ERECT   raeran i
ERR   dwolian ii; dysigian ii
ERRAND   aerende (aerendu) n.
ERROR   dwield (-) n.; dwola (-n) m.; slide
    (slidas) m.
ESCAPE   diegan i; losian ii; slupan 2; swican i
ESTABLISH   regnian ii; settan i; staðolian ii;
    staelan i
ESTATE   weorðig (-as) m.
ESTATE, INHERITED   eðel (eðlas) m.
ESTEEM   eahtle (eahtlan) f.
ESTEEM   eahtian ii; weorðian ii
ESTEEMED   weorð
ESTUARY   hyð (-a) f.; muða (-n) m.
ETERNAL   ece
EVACUATION (FROM THE BODY)   utfor (-a) f.
EVE   aefen (-) n.
EVEN   efene; furðum
EVEN WITH   efen
EVENING   aefen (-) n.; tweoneleoht (-) n.
EVENT   byre (byras) m.; wyrd (-e) f.
EVER   a; aefre

26

EVERYONE   aeghwaeđer
EVERYTHING   eall
EVERYWHERE   aeghwaer; gehwaer
EVIDENCE   segn (-as, -) m. n.; tacen (-) n.
EVIDENT   cnaewe; sweotol; undierne
EVIL   atol (-) n.; bealu (-) n.; leahtor m.;
    trag (-a) f.
EVIL   yfel
EVILLY   trage
EXACTLY   furđum
EXAMPLE   bysen (bysna) f.; waefersyn (-e) f.
EXASPERATE   tiergan i
EXCELLENCE   duguđ (-a) f.; fremu (frema) f.
EXCELLENT   cyst; freme; wraest
EXCELLENTLY   wraeste
EXCEPT   butan; nefne
EXCESS   ormaetnes (-a) f.
EXCESSIVE   ofer- pref.
EXCHANGE   gewrixle (gewrixlu) n.; wrixl (-a) f.
EXCHANGE   wrixlan i
EXCHANGE FOR   mutian ii
EXCITE   drefan i; wregan i
EXCREMENT   utgang (-as) m.
EXCUSE   ladian ii
EXECUTE (DO)   hiegan i; laestan i
EXECUTIONER   cwellere (cwelleras) m.
EXHAUST   besylcan i; waecan i
EXHORT   manian ii
EXILE   wrecca (-n) m.
EXILE   draefan i
EXISTENCE   wist (-a) f.
EXPECT   hopian ii; wenan i
EXPECTATION   wen (-e) f.
EXPEDITION   faer (faru) n.
EXPERIENCE   dreogan 2
EXPERIENCED   frod
EXPLOIT   siđ (-as) m.
EXPLORE   neosian ii; rasian ii
EXPOSE   berian i; sceawian ii
EXPOSED   baer
EXPOUND   reccan i; trahtian ii
EXTEND   reccan i; streccan i; đenian i
EXTENSIVE   sid ; wid
EXTENSIVELY   side; wide
EXTINGUISH   dwaescan i; acwencan i

EXTOL   maersian ii
EXTRA   oðer; unnydlic
EXULT   hreman i; hreðan i
EXULTANT   hremig
EYE   eage (eagan) n.
EYELASH   bru (-a) f.

F

FACE   hleor (-) n.; wlita (-n) m.
FACE TO FACE   eawunga
FACING   toweard
FAIR   beorht; cyme; cyrten; faeger; sciene
FAITH   geleafa (-n) m.; waer f.
FAITHFUL   faele; hold
FAITHFULLY   faele
FALCON   hafoc (-as) m.
FALL   dryre m.; fiell (-as) m.; hryre m.
FALL   dreosan 2; feallan 7; hreosan 2; stregdan 3
FALL IN BATTLE   cringan 3; licgan i-5
FALLING   dreorung (-a) f.
FALSE   leas; lysu; sleac; unhold
FALSEHOOD   leas (-) n.; leasung (-a) f.; lyge
    (-as, -) m. n.; lygen (-a) f.
FALSIFY   leogan 2
FAME   blaed (-as) m.; dom (-as) m.; hlisa m.;
    hreð n.; maerðu (maerða) f.
FAMILIAR   cuð
FAMILY   cnosl n.; cynd (-e, -) f. n.; cynn (-)
    n.; heord (-a) f.
FAMILY MEMBERS   hiwan m. pl.
FAMOUS   breme; gefraege
FAR   feorr
FAR AWAY   rume av.
FARE   faersceatt (-as) m.
FARMSTEAD   weorðig (-as) m.; wic (-) n.
FASTEN   faestnian ii; spannan 7
FASTNESS   faesten (-) n.
FAT   gelynd f.; smeoru (-) n.
FAT   ðiccol
FATE   gifeðe n.; meotod m.; wyrd (-e) f.
FATED TO DIE   faege; witod
FATHER   faeder (-) m.
FATHER-CONFESSOR   scrift (-as) m.
FAULT   culpe (culpan) f.; gylt (-as) m.

28

FAVOR   ar (-a) f.; est (-e) f.; liss/liðs (-a)
    f.; milds (-a) f.
FAVORITE   dierling (-as) m.
FEAR   ege m.; forhtung (-a) f.; oga (-n) m.
FEAR   fyrhtan i; onegan i
FEARFUL   ag- pref.; forhtful; ongrislic
FEARSOME   ag- pref.
FEAST   swaesendu n. pl.; symbel (-) n.
FEAST   symblian ii
FEATHER   feðer (-a) f.
FEATHER   feðerian ii; feðrian ii
FED UP WITH   saed
FEED   fedan i; feormian ii; leppan i
FEEL   felan i
FELL   fiellan i
FEN   fenn (-as) m.; mor (-as) m.
FENNEL   finol m.
FERMENT   daerst(e) f.
FERN   fearn (-) n.
FETTER   band (-as, -a) m. f.; bind (-) n.; haeft
    (-as) m.; hring (-as) m.; lann (-a) f.;
    wrasen (wrasna) f.
FETTERS   fetera f. pl.; wriðan m. pl.
FETTER   cyspan i; feterian ii; haeftan i
FEUD   faehð(u) (faehða) f.
FEVER   fefer (-) m. n.
FEW   fea; lyt
FEW, A   fea; hwon; lyt; lythwon
FIDELITY   holdsciepe (holdsciepan) m.; treow
    (-a) f.
FIELD, CULTIVATED   aecer (-as) m.
FIEND (SATAN)   feond (-as, fiend) m.
FIERCE   afor; fell; grimm; reoc; wilde; wrað
FIERY   fyren
FIFTEEN   fiftiene
FIFTH   fifta
FIFTY   fiftig
FIGHT   camp (-as) m.; feoht (-) n.; feohte
    (feohta) f.; fitt n.; tohte (tohtan) f.
FIGHT   feohtan 3; lacan 7; plegan i; wigan i
FIGHT FOR   campian ii
FIGHTER   cempa (-n) m.
FILE   feol (-a) f.
FILL   fyllað n.
FILL OF FOOD   fyllu f.

```
FILL      fyllan i
FILTH     fylð f.; horh (horas) m.; widl (-as) m.
FIND      findan 3; metan i
FIND OUT      cunian ii; geascian ii
FIND      -fynde suff.
FINGER    finger (fingras) m.
FIRE      aeled m.; bael n.; fyr (-) n.
FIRM      trum
FIRM IN      -faest suff.
FIRMLY    faeste; wraeste
FIRST     frum- pref.
FIRST     forma; fyrmesta
FIRST, AT      aerest
FISH      fisc (-as) m.
FIST      fyst (-a) f.
FITTING      fog (-) n.
FITTING      behefe; gemet; risne
FITTING, BE      risan 1
FIT TOGETHER      fegan i
FIVE      fif
FIXED     faest
FIXED IN      -faest suff.
FIXEDLY      faeste
FLAG      fana (-n) m.
FLAME     ad (-as) m.; bael n.; brand (-as) m.;
     lieg (-as) m.
FLAMES    sweolað m. n.
FLAMING      ligen
FLASH     breahtm (-as) m.
FLASH OF LIGHTNING      liget (-ta, -tu) f. n.
FLASHING      ligen
FLATTER      oleccan i
FLATTERY      olaecung (-a) f.
FLAX      fleax n.; lin n.
FLAY      flean 6; holdian ii
FLEE      fleon 2
FLEECE      flies n.
FLESH     flaesc n.; hnesce (-) n.
FLIER      -flaga (-n) m. suff.
FLIES     mysci n. pl.
FLIGHT, PUT TO      flieman i
FLIGHT OF A BIRD      flyge m.; flyht (-as) m.
FLIGHT TO SAFETY      fleam (-as) m.
FLINT     flint (-as) m.
FLOAT     fleotan 2; swimman 3
```

```
FLOATER    flota (-n) m.
FLOCK    heord (-a) f.
FLOCK OF SHEEP    eowde f.
FLOOD    flod (-as) m.
FLOOR    flor (-as) m.; scielfe (scielfa) f.
FLOOR (HALL OR COMMON ROOM)    flett (-) n.
FLOURISH    blowan 7; rogian ii; spedan i
FLOW    gyte m.
FLOW    flowan 7; geotan 2; rinnan 3
FLOW OUT    ebbian ii
FLUCTUATE    wafian ii; ydian ii
FLY    fleoge (fleogan) f.
FLY    fleogan 2
FLYING    flacor
FOAM    fam n.
FOAM    famigan ii; faeman i
FOAMY    famig
FOE    lad (-) n.; scada (-n) m.
FOLD    fealdan 7
FOLD    -feald suff.
FOLIAGE    bled (-a) f.; leafu n. pl.
FOLLOW    folgian ii; fylgan i
FOLLOW AFTER    ehtan i
FOLLOW IN THE TRACK OF    spyrian ii
FOLLOWERS    folgere (folgeras) m.
FOLLOWING    folgad (-as) m.
FOMENT    bedian ii
FOOD    aet m. f.; fodor m.; fostor m.; lifen (-a)
    f.; mete (mettas) m.; mos (-) n.; reord(e)
    (reordu) n.; swaesendu n. pl.; digen f.; wist
    (-a) f.
FOOLISH    dol; dwaes; dysig
FOOLISHLY, ACT    dysigian ii
FOOLISHNESS    gead (-a) f.
FOOT    fot (fet) m.
FOOTPRINT    fotlast (-as) m.
FOOT-SOLDIER    feda (-n) m.
FOOTSTOOL    fotsceamol (-as) m.
FOR    for
FORCE    bad f.; dryht (-a) f.; trum (-) n.
FORCE    niedan i
FORD    waed (wadu) n.
FOREIGN    eldeodig; fremde/frem(e)de
FOREMOST    forma; fyrmesta
FORERUNNER    forerynel (-as) m.
```

31

FOREST   weald (-as) m.
FORGET   forgietan 5; ofergietan 5
FORGETFUL   ofergietel
FORGETFULNESS   ofergietnes f.
FORGIVE   forgiefan 5
FORM   hiew (-) n.; lic (-) n.
FORM   hiewan i
FORNICATION   forliger n.
FORNICATOR   haemend (-) m.
FORSAKE   forlaetan 7
FORTHWITH   samnunga/semnunga
FORTUNE   saeld (-a) f.
FORTUNATE   eadig
FORTY   feowertig
FORWARD   foran av. prep.; ford; gegnum
FOUL   ful
FOUND   staelan i
FOUNDATION   stadol (-as) m.; trum (-) n.
FOUNDER   settend (-as) m.
FOUNTAIN   wiell (-as) m.; wiella (-n) m.; wielle
    (wiellan) f.
FOUR   feower
FOURTEEN   feowertiene
FOURTH   feo(we)rda
FOX   fox (-as) m.
FRAGILE   bryce
FRAGRANCE   swaece (swaccas) m.
FRAIL   tydre; wac
FRANKLY   untraglice
FREE   freo; tom
FREEDOM   freodom (-as) m.; frignes (-a) f.
FREEMAN   ceorl (-as) m.
FREE-WILL   freodom (-as) m.
FREEZE   colian ii; freosan 2
FREEZING COLD   freorig
FREIGHT   fearm (-as) m.
FREQUENT   neosan i; neosian ii
FRESH   fersc
FRIDAY   Frigedaeg (Frigedagas) m.
FRIEND   freond (-as, friend) m.; wine (-as, -)
    m.
FRIENDLY   lide; som
FRIENDLY, BECOME   lidian ii
FRIENDSHIP   sibb (-a) f.
FRIGHT   fyrhtu (fyrhta) f.

FRIGHTEN   aclian ii; faeran i; gaestan i; onegan
    i
FRIGHTENED, BECOME   forhtian ii
FRIGHTENED   acol; forht; forhtig; fyrht
FRINGE   fnaed (fnadu) n.
FRINGE OF A GARMENT   wloh (-) n.
FROG   tosca (-n) m.
FROM   aet; of prep.; on av.
FRONT OF, IN   foran av. prep.
FRONT RANK   ord (-) n.
FROST   forst (-as) m.
FRUIT   bled (-a) f.; ofett n.; waestm (-as, -a)
    m. f.
FUGITIVE   fliema (-n) m.
FULFILL   fullian ii; fyllan i
FULL OF   full; -full suff.; saed
FUNCTION   ambiht (-u) n.
FURNACE   ofen (-as) m.
FURNISH   teo(ga)n ii
FURTHER   furdor; gen; dagen
FURTHER   fyrdran i
FURTHERMORE   ma
FURZE   fyrs (-as) m.
FUTURE, TOWARD THE   foreweard

G

GABLE   horn (-as) m.
GAIETY   bliss (-a) f.; dream (-as) m.
GAIT   fede n.; gang (-as) m.; stepe (stapas) m.
GALLOWS   gealga (-n) m.
GAME-BAG   glof (-a) f.
GANG-PLANK   bolca (-n) m.
GANNET   ganot (-as) m.
GAPE   ganian ii; ginan 1
GARMENT   gierela (-n) m.; hraegel (-) n.; reaf
    (-) n.; waed (-a) f.
GATE   dor (-u) n.; duru (dura) f.; geat (-u) n.;
    port (-as) m.
GATHER   gadrian ii; samnian ii
GEM   gimm (-as) m.
GENERAL   heretoga (-n) m.
GENERATE   edbyrdan i
GENERATION   cneoriss (-a) f.; cneorisn (-a) f.
GENEROUS   freo; milde; ungniede

GENITALS   maegðblaed (-u) n.; scamu (scama) f.
GENTLE   bleað; hnesce; liðe; milde; smolt
GENTLY   sefte; smolte; softe
GET   begietan 5; strienan i
GIANT   ent (-as) m.; eoten (-as) m.; gigant (-as)
    m.; ðyrs (-as) m.
GIFT   gifu n.; forgiefnes (-a) f.; lac (-a, -)
    f. n.; laen f. n.
GIGANTIC   entisc; eotenisc
GILDED   gylden
GIRD   gyrdan i
GIVE   forgiefan 5; giefan 5; leon 1; sellan i
GIVE WAY   swican 1
GIVEN   giefeðe
GIVER   giefa (-n) m.; sellend (-as) m.
GLAD   faegen
GLADDEN   retan i; taetan i
GLASS   glaes n.
GLEAM   leoma (-n) m.
GLEAM   liexan i
GLIDE   scriðan 1
GLISTEN   glisnian ii; glitenian ii
GLISTENING   brun
GLORIFY   diersian ii; domian ii; maeran i; wul-
    drian ii
GLORY   blaed (-as) m.; gielp m.; hreð n.; maerðu
    (maerða) f.; tir (-as) m.; ðrymm (-as) m.;
    wuldor (-) n.
GLORY   hreðan i
GLOW   glowan 7
GLUTTON   gifer (-as) m.
GNASH   gristbitian ii
GNAT   gnaett (-as) m.
GNAW   gnagan 6
GO   cuman 4; faran 6; feran i; gan anv.; gangan
    7; gengan i; gewitan 1; leoran i, ii-2;
    liðan 1; strican 1; wadan 6; wendan i
GO FORWARD   steppan 6
GO UP (OR DOWN)   stigan 1
GOAD   gad f.
GOD   Demend m.; God m.; Meotod m.; Stierend m.
GOD (PAGAN)   god (-u) n.
GODDESS   gyden (-a) f.
GOING   stepe (stapas) m.; wað f.
GOLD   gold (-) n.

GOLDEN   gylden
GOOD   cystig; faele; freme; god; til
GOOD IN COUNCIL   rynig
GOOD, BE   dugan prp.
GOODNESS   fremu (frema) f.
GOOSE   gos (ges) f.
GORE   dreor m.
GORGE   ceole (ceolan) f.; hrace (hracan) f.
GORY   dreorig
GOVERN   racian ii; wealdan 7
GRACE   ar (-a) f.; est (-e) f.; giefnes (-a) f.;
    liss/liðs (-a) f.
GRACEFUL   smael
GRACIOUS   este; estig; fremsum; glaed; liðe
GRAIN   corn n.
GRAMMAR   staefcraeft (-as) m.
GRANDSON   nefa (-n) m.
GRANT   laenan i; leon 1; ðafian ii; unnan prp.
GRANTED   eaden
GRASP   feng (-as) m.; grap (-a) f.; gripe m.
GRASP   fon 7; grapian ii; gripan i
GRASS   graes n.
GRATIFY   lician ii
GRAVE   byrgen (brygna) f.; graef (grafu) n.;
    hoðma (-n) m.
GRAVEDIGGER   byrgend (-as) m.
GRAVEN IMAGE   graeft m. f. n.
GRAY   graeg; har; hasu
GREEDY   frec; gifre; graedig
GREEN   grene
GREET   gretan i; haelsian ii
GRIEF   breð (-a) f.; gehðu (gehða) f.; gnornung
    (-a) f.; gnorn (-as) m.; gnyrn (-a) f.; heaf
    m.; hearm (-as) m.; torn (-) n.; trega (-n)
    m.
GRIEF, COME TO   breoðan 2
GRIEVE   eglan i; gnorian ii; heofan i-7; sargian
    ii; sorgian ii
GRIEVING   sorgung (-a) f.
GRIEVIOUS   sar; swaer; treaflic
GRIMACE   grennian ii
GRIN   grennian ii
GRIND   grindan 3
GRIP   clamm (-as) m.; feng (-as) m.; grap (-a)
    f.; gripe m.

35

GRIP   gripan 1
GRISLY   ongrislic
GROAN   granian ii; maenan i
GROUND   grund (-as) m.
GROUP   gemang (-) n.; genge (gengan) f.
GROVE   bearu (bearwas) m.; holt (-) n.
GROW   alan 6; leodan 2; weaxan 7
GROW LARGE   eacnian ii; miclian ii
GROWTH   wacor f.; waestm (-as, -a) m. f.
GUARD   warian ii; weardian ii
GUARDIAN   weard (-as) m.
GUARDIANSHIP   weard (-a) f.
GUEST   gast-/gaest- pref.; giest (-as) m.
GUIDANCE   steor (-a) f.
GUIDE   stierend m.; wisa (-n) m.
GUIDE   stieran i
GUILE   list (-as) m.; lot (-u) n.
GUILEFUL, BECOME   lytigian ii
GUILT   gylt (-as) m.; scyld (-a) f.
GUILTY   gyltig; scyldig
GUILTY, BE   gyltan i

H

HABIT   đeaw (-as) m.; wrena (-n) m.
HABITUAL   gewunelic
HAIL   hagol/haegel (haeglas) m. n.
HAIR   feax n.; haer (-) n.
HAIRED   -feax suff.
HAIRY   haere; loccod; ruh
HALF   healf (-a) f.
HALF   healf
HALF-NAKED   healfnacod
HALF-YEAR   missere (misseru) n.
HALL   heall (-a) f.; reced (-as) m.; salor (-)
    n.; sael (salu) n.; seld (-) n.; sile (-) m.
HALLOW   halgian ii
HALT   bid n.
HALT   healt
HAMMER   hamor (-as) m.
HAMSTRING   hamelian ii
HAND   clamm (-as) m.; folm (-a) f.; hand (-a) f.;
    mund (-a) f.
HAND, AT   gehende
HANDSOME   anlic

HANG   hangian ii intrans.; hon 7 trans.
HANGING THING   hangele (hangellan) f.
HAPPEN   byrian i; limpan 3; saelan i; sceon i
HAPPEN FOR THE FIRST TIME   niewian ii
HAPPENING   byre (byras) m.; gelimp (-u) n.
HAPPILY   bliđe
HAPPINESS   bliss (-a) f.; dream (-as) m.
HAPPY   bliđe; eadig; gal; glaed; saelig; tat
HARBOR   hyđ (-a) f.
HARD   enge; heard; sliđe(n); stiđ
HARDEN   hierdan i; stielan i
HARDSHIP   earfođ (-u) n.
HARKEN   hearcnian ii
HARM   bealu (-) n.; byrst (-as) m.; daru (dara)
    f.; gryn (-as, -) m. n.; laeđđe f.; lyre
    (-as) m.; teosu (teosa) f.
HARM   derian ii; mierran i; scieđđan i-6; teos-
    wian ii
HARNESS   baetan i
HARP   hearpe (hearpan) f.
HARPIST   hearpere (hearperas) m.
HARRY   hergian ii
HARSH   geocor
HART   heorot (-as) m.
HARVEST   haerfest (-as) m.; rip (-u) n.
HARVEST   ripan 1
HARVEST SEASON   haerfest (-as) m.
HASTE   ofost (-a) f.
HASTEN   fysan i; onettan i; efstan i; scyndan i;
    sneowan 7; snierian i; tengan i
HAT   haett (-as) m.
HATCHET   adesa (-n) m.
HATE   hete m.
HATE   feo(ga)n i; hatian ii
HATEFUL   egle; fracuđ; lađwende
HATRED   hete m.
HAVE   agan prp.; habban iii; nabban iii neg.
HAVE TO   sculan prp.
HAWK   hafoc (-as) m.
HAY   hieg n.
HE WHO   se đe
HEAD   hafola (-n) m.; heafod (heafdas) m.
HEADLAND   naess (-as) m.
HEAL   haelan i
HEALER   haelend (-) m.

HEALING   halwende
HEALTH   hael(u) f.
HEALTH, GOOD   snytu (snyta) f.
HEALTHY   sund
HEAP   heap (-as) m.
HEAR   hearcnian ii; hieran i; hlystan i
HEARING   hlyst f.
HEART   breost (-) n.; heorte (heortan) f.;
    hreðer (-as) m.; sefa (-n) m.
HEARTBREAK   brecð (-a) f.
HEARTED   -heort suff.
HEARTEN   hiertan i
HEARTH   heorð (-as) m.
HEAT   haete f.; sweoloð m. n.; swol n.
HEAT   haetan i
HEATH   haeð m. n.
HEATHEN   haeðen
HEAVEN   heofon (-as) m.; rodor (-as) m.
HEAVEN, COMING FROM   heofoncund
HEAVENLY   heofonlic(e)
HEAVY   hefig; saed; swancor
HEDGEHOGS   erinaces pl.
HEED   giemen (-a) f.
HEED   hedan i
HEEL   hoh (hoas) m.
HEIGHT   hiehðu (hiehða) f.; ypplen (-u) n.
HEIR   eafora (-n) m.; ierfa (-n) m.; ierfnuma
    (-n) m.
HELL   hell f.
HELMET   helm (-as) m.
HELP   frofor (frofra) f.; fultum m.; fylst m. f.;
    help (-as, -a) m. f.; geoc (-a) f.; raed
    (-as) m.
HELP   frefran i; fultumian ii; fylstan i;geocian
    ii; helpan 3
HELPER   geocend (-) m.; helpend (-) m.
HEMP   haenep m.
HENCE   hinan
HERALD   fricca (-n) m.
HERB   wyrt (-a) f.
HERD   heord (-a) f.
HERDER   hierde (hierdas) m.
HERE   her
HERE, FROM   hinan
HERESY   dwield (-) n.; dwola (-n) m.

38

HERETIC   gedwolmann (gedwolmenn) m.
HESITATE   tweo(ga)n ii; wandian ii
HEW   heawan 7
HIDDEN   dierne
HIDE   deagan 7; dieglan i; helan 4; hydan i;
    wreon i
HIDING   heolstor (heolstras) m.
HIGH   heah; steap
HIGH, STAND   hlifian ii
HIGHER   ufor
HILL   beorg (-as) m.; cnoll (-as) m.; dun (-a)
    f.; hlinc (-as) m.; hyll (-as, -a) m. f.
HILLS   geswieru n. pl.
HILL, FROM A   ofdune
HILLSIDE   hlið (-u, -) n.
HILT   hilt (-as) m.
HILTED   hilted
HIND   hind (-a) f.
HINDER   dwellan i; gaelan i; lemman i; lettan i;
    twaefan i
HINDMOST   hindema
HINDRANCE   meorring (-a) f.
HIP   hype (hypas) m.
HIRE   hyr (-a) f.
HIRE   ahyrian ii
HISS   hwinan 1
HITHER   hider
HOAR-FROST   hrim m.
HOAR-FROST, COVERED WITH   hrimig
HOARY   har
HOCK   hoh (hoas) m.
HOLD   hafenian ii; healdan 7
HOLD IN THE HAND   hendan i
HOLE   pytt (-as) m.; sead (-as) m.
HOLLOW   hol
HOLLOW IN THE GROUND   hol (-u) n.
HOLY   halig; sanct
HOME   cudd(u) (cydda) f.; eard (-as) m.; ham
    (-as) m.
HONEST   treowe; unorne
HONEY   huneg m.
HONEY-DEW   meledeaw m.
HONOR   ar (-a) f.; gleng (-a) f.; dyncdo (dync-
    da) f.; tir (-as) m.; weordung (-a) f.
HONOR   arian ii; weordian ii

39

HOOD   hod m.
HOOD   -had suff.
HOP   hoppettan i
HOPE   hopa (-n) m.; hyht (-e) m.
HOPE   hopian ii; hyhtan i; treowan i
HOPELESS   orwene; wansaelig
HOPPER   hoppa (-n) m.
HORN   horn (-as) m.
HORRIBLE   atol
HORROR   oncyðð (-a) f.
HORSE   hors (-) m.; mearh (-as) m.; steda (-n) m.
HORSE, WHITE   blanca (-n) m.
HORSEMEN, BAND OF   eorod n.
HORSE-SHOE EDGED   calcrand
HOST   husl (-) n.
HOSTAGE   gisl (-as) m.
HOSTILE   fah; flah; hetlen; lað; orlege; wrað
HOSTILITY   faehð(u) (faehða) f.
HOT   hat; hatwende
HOT, MAKE   gledan i
HOUR   hwil (-a) f.; tid (-a) f.
HOUSE   hus (-) n.; sele (-) m.
HOUSEHOLD MEMBERS (LAY OR MONASTIC) hiwan m. pl.
HOVER   seomian ii
HOW   hu
HOWEVER   gehwaeðere av.; hwaeðere av.; ðeah av.
    conj.; ðeahna conj.
HOWL   ðeotan 2
HUMAN   mennisc
HUMAN BEING   mann
HUMANS   ielde m. pl.
HUMBLE   hnaegan i
HUMILIATE   hienan i; niðerian ii
HUMILIATION   hienð(u) (hienða) f.
HUNDRED   hund n.; hundred n.
HUNDRED TWENTY   hundtwelftig
HUNGER   graed (-as) m.; hungor m.
HUNGER   hyngran i
HUNGRY   hungrig
HUNT   huntian ii
HUNTING   huntoð m.
HUNTSMAN   hunta (-n) m.
HURRY   scudan 2
HURT   acan 6
HUSBANDMAN   ceorl (-as) m.

HYMN   ymen (-as) m.
HYSSOP   ysope f.

I

ICE   is n.
IDOL   wih/wioh (wios) m.
IF   gif; ðaer
ILLNESS   adl (-a) f.; suht (-a) f.
ILL-TREAT   tucian ii
ILLUMINATE   liehtan i
ILLUMINATION   liehtung (-a) f.
ILLUSTRIOUS   breme; maere
IMITATE   onhyrian i
IMMEDIATELY   gegnunga; sona
IMMERSE   diefan i; dyppan i
IMPEL   fysan i
IMPENDING   onsaege
IMPORTUNATE   mah
IMPROVE   betan i; godian ii
IMPURE   ful; unsyfre
IMPURITY   fylð f.; widl (-as) m.
IN   in prep.; inne av.; on prep.
INCANTATION   gealdor (gealdru) n.
INCENSE   riecels n.
INCITE   bryrdan i; hwettan i; tyhtan i
INCLINE   hieldan i; hlinian ii
INCLINED   niðerheald; niðerweard
INCLINED TO   -henge suff.
INCLINING   -heald suff.
INCREASE   eaca (-n) m.
INCREASE   iecan i; micelian ii; weaxan 7
INDEED   gear(w)e; huru
INDICATION   beacnung (-a) f.
INFAMY   aeswic (-as) m.
INFANTRYMAN   feða (-n) m.
INFERIOR   yfel
INFIRMITY   adl (-a) f.; medtrymnes (-a) f.
INFORMATION   gefraege n.
INFORMER   melda (-n) m.
INHERITANCE   ierfe n.; laf (-e) f.
INJURE   derian ii; scieððan i-6; teonian ii;
    yfelian ii
INJURIOUS   teon- pref.
INJURY   teosu (teosa) f.

INK   bocblaec n.
INNER   inna; innera; inneweard
INNOCENT   bilewit; unscaedig
INQUIRE   frecgan i-5; frigan 3
INQUIRING   frymlig
INQUIRY   ascung (-a) f.; aesce (aescan) f.
INSCRIBE   writan 1
INSECT   ceafor (-as) m.
INSECT, FLYING   fleoge (fleogan) f.
INSERT   don anv.
INSIDE   inn(e); innan
INSIDES   innod m. f.
INSPECT   sceawian ii
INSPECTION   sceawung (-a) f.
INSTRUCT   taecan i
INSTRUCTION   lar (-a) f.; tyht m.
INSULT   bismer m. f. n.; hosp (-as) m.
INTACT   onwealg
INTELLIGENCE   andgiet n.; witt n.
INTEND   mynian ii; myntan i
INTENT   hyht (-e) m.; hyge (-) m.
INTENTION   (in)gehygd (-u) f. n.; man (-a) f.
INTERCOURSE   gemana (-n) m.
INTERCOURSE WITH, HAVE   haeman i; mengan i
INTERIOR   innera; innod
INTERIOR OF A HALL   heod (-a) f.
INTERVAL OF TIME   faec (facu) n.
INTREPID   ungeblyged
INVENT   findan 3
INVITATION   ladu (lada) f.
INVITE   ladian ii; dingan i
IRON   iren/isen/isern (-) n.
ISLAND   ieg (-a) f.; iegland (-) n.
ISSUED FROM   bewaden
IT WHICH   se de

J

JACKASS   assa (-n) m.
JAW   ceafl (-as) m.
JAWBONE   cinnban (-) n.
JAWS   geagl (-as) m.; goma (-n) m.
JEWEL   gimm (-as) m.
JEWELRY   beagas m. pl.
JEWELS, SET WITH   staenan i

JOIN   fegan i; tengan i; điedan i
JOINT   fog (-) n.
JOURNEY   faereld (-u) n.; fering (-a) f.; gang
     (-as) m.; rad (-a) f.; siđ (-as) m.
JOURNEY   faran 6; feran i; liđan 1; siđian ii
JOY   fea (-n) m.; gleo/glieg (-) n.; hrođor
     (hrođras) m.; hyht (-e) m.; lust (-as) m.;
     myrgđ (-a) f.; retu (reta) f.; sael (-e) m.
     wynn (-a) f.
JOYOUS   myrge(n)
JUDGE   dema (-n) m.
JUDGE   deman i
JUDGMENT DAY   dom (-as) m.
JUICE   seaw (-as) m.; wos n.
JUMP   hliep (-as) m.; stiell (-as) m.
JUMP   hleapan 7; hoppettan i; lacan 7; springan
     3; stiellan i
JUST   rihtlic
JUST   efene av.
JUST AS   furđum av.
JUSTLY   rihte

K

KEEN   hwaet
KEEP   healdan 7; weardian ii
KEEPING   weard (-a) f.
KEEP ON   forđ
KEY   caeg (caega) f.; caege (caegan) f.
KICK   spurnan 3
KILL   cwellan i; cwielman i; fiellan i; heawan 7;
     slean 6; spillan i; stierfan i
KILLING   cwalu f.; cwealm (-as) m.
KIND   freme; fremsum; milde
KINDLE   aelan i; gledan i
KINDLY   estig; mildelic
KINDNESS   fremu (frema) f.
KING   cyning (-as) n.
KINSMAN   magu (maga) m.; maecg (-as) m.; maecga
     (-n) m.; maeg (magas) m.
KISS   coss (-as) m.
KISS   cyssan i
KITCHEN   cycene (cycenan) f.
KITE (BIRD OF PREY)   cyta (-n) m.
KNEE   cneo (-) n.

43

KNOCK   cnossian ii
KNOCK AGAINST   cynssan i
KNOLL   cnoll (-as) m.
KNOW   cnawan 7; cunnan prp.; nytan prp. neg.;
    snytrian ii; witan prp.
KNOWN, MAKE   cyđan i
KNOWN   cuđ; gefraege
KNOWING   cyđig; gleaw
KNOWLEDGE   gefraege n.

L

LABOR   swinc (-) n.; đroht m.
LABOR   swencan i; swincan 3
LABORIOUS   đroht; đrohtig
LACK   gad/gaed n.; wan n.; wana (-n) m.
LACK   wanian ii
LACKING   leas;-leas suff.; orfierme; wan
LADDER   hlaeder (hlaedra) f.
LADY   frowe (frowan) f.; hlaefdige (hlaefdigan)
    f.; ides (-a) f.
LAIR   denn (-) n.; leger (-u) n.
LAKE   mere m.
LAMB   lamb(or) (lambru) n.
LAME   healt; lama
LAME PERSON   hinca (-n) m.
LAMENT   man (-a) f.; sorgleođ (-a) f.
LAMENT   cwanian ii; cwiđan i; geornian ii; greo-
    tan 2; heofan i-7; maenan i; sifian ii;
    wepan 7
LAMENTATION   gnornung (-a) f.; sifung (-a) f.
LAMENTING   wopig
LAMP   leohtfaet (leohtfatu) n.
LAND   eard (-as) m.; land (-) n.
LAND, ARABLE   aecer (-as) m.
LAND, NATIVE   cyđđu (cyđđa) f.; eđel (eđlas) m.
LAND A BOAT   lendan i
LANDING PLACE   hyđ (-a) f.
LANGUAGE   reord (-a) f.; tunge (tungan) f.; đeod-
    isc n.
LANTERN   blacern n.; olfaet (olfatu) n.
LAP   bearm (-as) m.; sceat (-as) m.
LARGE   eacen; micel
LATE   siđ av.; ufor av.
LATER   siđra av.; uferra av.; ufor av.

LATER (AGAIN)   eft
LAUGH   hliehhan i-6
LAUGHTER   hleahtor m.
LAW (ETERNAL)   ae f.
LAW (JUSTICE, PRINCIPLE, CUSTOM)   riht (-) n.
LAW (LEGAL)   lagu (laga) f.
LAW (MEASURE, STANDARD)   gemet (-u) n.
LAY (POEM)   giedd (-) n.
LAY   lecgan i
LAY (MAN)   laewede
LAY WASTE   ieđan i
LAZY   sleac
LEAD   lead n.
LEAD   laedan i
LEADER   fruma (-n) m.; raeswa (-n) m.; wisa (-n)
     m.
LEADER (ARMY)   heretoga (-n) m.
LEADER (TEACHER)   latteow (-as) m.
LEAF   blaed (bladu) n.; leaf (-) n.
LEAN, CAUSE TO   hlaenan i
LEAP   hliep (-as) m.; stiell (-as) m.
LEAP   hleapan 7; hoppettan i; stiellan i
LEARN   frignan 3; leornian ii
LEARNER   leornere (leorneras) m.
LEARNING   leornung f.
LEATHER   leđer (-u) n.
LEAVE   leaf (-a) f.
LEAVE BEHIND   laefan i
LEAVEN   daerst(e) f.
LEAVINGS   laf (-as) m.
LECHERY   gal n.; galnes f.
LEE OF, IN   under prep.
LEFT   winestre
LEFT HAND   winestre f.
LEND   laenan i
LENGTH   lengu f.
LENGTHEN   lengan i
LEPEROUS   hreaf
LESS   wan- pref.
LESSEN   lytlian ii; minsian ii; wanian ii
LET   laetan 7
LETTUCE   leahtric m.
LETTER-MESSAGE   epistola (-n) m.
LEVEL   efen
LIAR   -loga (-n) m. suff.

45

LIBRARY   bocgesamnung (-a) f.
LICK   liccian ii
LID   hlid (-u) n.
LIE   lyge (-as, -) m. n.
LIE, TELL A   leogan 2
LIE DOWN   licgan i-5
LIE DOWN DEAD   licgan i-5
LIE IN WAIT FOR   saetan i
LIE TO, GIVE THE   leogan 2
LIFE   droht m. n.; ealdor (-) n.; feorh (feoras,
    -) m. n.; ferhđ (-as, -) m. n.; lif (-) n.
LIFE, WAY OF   drohtađ m.
LIFE, BRING INTO   cwician ii
LIFT   hebban i-6
LIGHT   candel (-a) f.; leoht n.; leoma (-n) m.;
    tapor (-as) m.
LIGHT   leoht; hwit
LIGHT (SHADE)   blac
LIGHT-UP   liehtan i
LIKE   lician ii
LIKE, CAUSE TO   lician ii
LIKE, MAKE TO BE   licettan i
LIKE (SIMILAR)   gelic
LIKEWISE   swelce av.
LILY   lilie (lilian) f.
LIMB   lim (-u) n.; liđ (-u) n.
LIMIT   gemet (-u) n.
LIMIT   mearcian ii
LIMITATION   gemet (-u) n.
LINDEN TREE   lind (-a) f.
LINDEN WOOD, MADE OF   linden
LINEAGE   ađelu f. n.; cyme (cymas) m.
LION   leo (-n) m.
LIONESS   leo (-n) f.
LIPS   welera f. pl.; weleras m. pl.
LISTEN   hlosnian ii
LISTEN TO   hlystan i; hieran i
LISTEN! (RHETORICAL COMMAND)   hwaet!; la!
LISTENING   hlyst f.
LITHE   swancor
LITTLE   lytel a.
LITTLE   fea av.; hwaene av.; hwon av.; lythwon
    av.
LIVE   gebidan 1; libban iii; lifian ii
LIVELY   horsc; liflic

LIVESTOCK   neat (-) n.
LIVESTOCK, SMALL   nieten (-) n.
LIVID   blat(e)
LIVING   cwic
LO!   hwaet!; la!
LOAD   hladan 6; hlaestan i
LOAF   hlaf (-as) m.
LOAM   lam m.
LOAMY   lamen
LOAN   laen (-u) n.
LOAN   laenan i
LOAN, ON   laene
LOATHLY   lað
LOCK   clustor (clustru) n.; loc (-u) n.; loca
    (-n) m.
LOCK OF HAIR   locc (-as) m.
LOCK   lucan 2
LONG   lang
LONG AGO   fyrn av.
LONG FOR   langian ii; lengian ii
LONG TIME, FOR A   lange av.
LONGING   langað (-as) m.; langung (-a) f.
LONG-LASTING   langsum
LOOK   locian ii; wlitan 1
LOOK AT   sceawian ii; starian ii
LOOSE   leas
LORD   brego m.; dryhten (dryhtnas) m.; ealdor
    (ealdras) m.; fengel (fenglas) m.; frea (-n)
    m.; hearra (-n) m.; hlaford (-as) m.; ðeoden
    (ðeodnas) m.; wine (-as, -) m.
LOSE   leosan 2
LOSE ONE'S WAY   losian ii
LOSS   lyre (-as) m.
LOT   hliet (-as) m.
LOT, OBTAIN BY   hleotan 2
LOTS, A CASTING OF   hlytm (-as) m.
LOUD   hlud
LOUDLY   hlude
LOVE   freod (-a) f.; lufu (lufa, lufan) f.
LOVE   freo(ga)n i; lufian ii
LOVELY   cyme; faeger
LOW   hean
LOWER   hienan i
LOWLY   hean; heanlic
LOYAL   hold; treowe

47

LOYALTY   hyldu f.; treowð (-a) f.
LUCKY   ead
LUMINOUS   hwit
LUMP OF METAL   clympre (clympras) m.
LURE   spanan 7

M

MACHINATION   searu (-) n.; swice m.
MAD   dwolic; wod
MAGIC   drycraeft (-as) m.
MAGICIAN   dry (-as) m.
MAID   maegden (-u) n.; men(n)en (-u) n.
MAIDSERVANT   ðigen (-u) f.
MAJESTY   ðrymm (-as) m.; ðryð (-e) f.
MAKE   efnan i; macian ii; wyrcan i-6
MALE   waepnedmann (waepnedmenn) m.; wer (-as) m.
MALICE   inwitt n.
MAN   man(n) (menn) m.; esne (esnas) m.
MAN (KINSMAN)   magu (maga) m.; maecg (-as) m.;
    maecga (-n) m.; maeg (magas) m.
MAN (MALE CREATURE)   waepnedmann (waepnedmenn)
    m.; wer (-as) m.
MAN (PERSON OF A NATION)   leod (-as) m.
MAN (WARRIOR)   haele (haeleðas) m.; haeleð (-)
    m.; scealc (-as) m.; secg (-as) m.
MAN, BOLD   bealdor m.; hearding (-as) m.
MAN, YOUNG   beorn (-as) m.
MANE   manu (mana) f.
MANGER   binn (-a) f.; cribb (-a) f.
MANLY   ðegnlice
MANIFEST   orgyte; yppe
MANNER   gecynde (gecyndu) n.; wise (wisan) f.
MANNERS   ðeaw (-as) m.
MANOR   ham (-as) m.
MANY   fela; manig
MANY A   manig
MAR   mierran i
MARK   mael (-) n.; mearc (-as) m.; miercels m.
    f.; segn (-) n.
MARK   taecnan i
MARKET   ceapstow (-a) f.
MARKET-TOWN   port (-as, -) m. n.
MARRIAGE   haemed n.; sinciepe (sinciepas) m.;
    wedlac (-) f. n.

MARRIAGE CEREMONY   bryd̄ing (-) n.
MARRY   haeman i; weddian ii
MARSH   fenn (-as, -) m. n.; merisc (-as) m.
MARTYR   martir (-as) m.; d̄rowere (d̄roweras) m.
MARVEL   waefd̄(u) (-a) f.; wundor (-) n.
MARVEL AT   wundrian ii
MASK   grima (-n) m.
MASS   maesse (maessan) f.
MAST   maest (-as) m.
MASTER   hearra (-n) m.; hlaford (-as) m.
MASTER (TEACHER)   magister (magistras) m.
MATERNAL   medren
MATTER   intinga (-n) m.
MAY   motan prp.
MEAD   me(o)du m.
MEAL   sand (-a) f.; wist (-a) f.
MEASURE   byden (-a) f.; gemet (-u) n.
MEASURE (BUSHEL)   mitta (-n) m.
MEASURE   metan 5
MEAT, ROAST   braeding (-a) f.
MEDIATE   geondd̄encan i; metgian ii
MEDIATION   metgung (-a) f.
MEDITATE   smeagan i
MEET   gretan i; metan i
MEETING   gemot (-) n.; maed̄el (-u) n.; metung
    (-a) f.
MEETING-PLACE   gemot (-) n.
MELODY   swegel n.; swinn m.; sweg (-as) m.; wise
    (wisa) f.
MELT   meltan 3
MELTING   geargnryne (geargnrynas) m.
MEMORY   gemynd (-a, -) f. n.; mynd (-a, -) f. n.
MEN (SEE MAN)   tudor (-) n.
MENTION   maenan i; namian ii
MERCIFUL, BE   mildsian ii
MERCY   milds (-a) f.; mildsung (-a) f.
MERIT   earnung (-a) f.
MERIT, EARN   earnian ii
MERRIMENT   beorscip (-an) m.; dream (-as) m.
    myrgd̄ (-a) f.
MERRY   myrge(n)
MERRY, BE   myrgan i
MESSAGE   aerende (aerendu) n.; bodung (-a) f.
MESSAGE, TAKE A   aerendian ii
MESSENGER   ambiht (-as) m.; ar (-as) m.; boda

MESSENGER (CONTD.)   (-n) m.; ferend (-) m.
METAL   iren
METAL, WORK   smiðian ii
METE OUT   daelan i; metan 5
MIDDAY   undern m.
MIDDLING   medeme
MIGHT   afal n.; maegen n.; meaht (-a) f.;
    strengu (strenge) f.
MIGHTY   meagol; mihtig; rice
MILD   milde; smylte; weðe
MILE   mil (-a) f.
MILITIA (DEFENDING)   fierd (-a) f.
MILK   meolc f.
MIND   ferhð (-as,-) m. n.; hygd (-u) f. n.; hyge
    m.; mod m.; mynd (-a, -) f. n.; ðanc (-as)
    m.; ðoht (-as) m.
MINDED   -hydig suff.; -mod suff.
MINDFUL   hydig; myndig
MINGLE   blandan 7; mengan i
MINGLING   gebland n.; gemang (-) n.
MINISTER (POLITICAL)   scealc (-as) m.; ðegn (-as)
    m.
MINISTER   ðegnian ii; ðeowian ii
MIRACLE   wundor (-) n.
MIRTH   gamen n.
MISERABLY   coðlice
MISERY   iermðu (iermða) f.; wraec n.
MISFORTUNE   daru (dara) f.; trega (-n) m.; wea
    (-n) m.
MISLEAD   dwellan i
MISLEADING   gedwolsum
MISS   missan i
MISSION (POLITICAL)   sand f.
MIST   mist (-as) m.
MISTREAT   hierwan i
MISTRESS (LADY OF THE HOUSE)   hlaefdige (hlaef-
    digan) f.
MISTY   mistig
MIX   blandan 7; gewrixlan i; mengan i
MOCK   bismerian ii; hyppan i
MOCKERY   bismer m. f. n.; husc (-as) m.
MODERATE (MITIGATE)   metgian ii
MODERATE   maete
MODERATION   metgung (-a) f.
MOISTURE   seaw (-as) m.; steam (-as) m.

MOLEST   eglan i; reafian ii
MOMENT   stund (-a) f.
MONASTERY   mynster (-u) n.
MONDAY   Monandaeg (Monandagas) m.
MONEY   mynet (-u) n.; scaett (-as) m.
MONEY-CHANGER   myntere (mynteras) m.
MONK   munuc (-as) m.
MONSTER   aglaeca (-n) m.
MONTH   calend (-as) m.; monað (-) m.
MOON   mona (-n) m.
MOON, FULL   waðol m.
MOPE   aswaeman i
MORE   ma n.
MORNING   mergen/morgen (morgnas) m.
MORNING, EARLY   aernmorgen (aernmorgnas) m.;
    uhta (-n) m.
MORNING, MID   undern m.
MORROW   mergen/morgen (morgnas) m.
MORSEL   giefl (-) n.; snaed (-as) m.
MOTH   moððe (moððan) f.
MOTHER   modor (-) f.
MOTION   tyht m.; wað f.
MOUNT   clymmian ii
MOUNTAIN   beorg (-as) m.; hleoð (-as) m.; munt
    (-as) m.
MOURN   murnan 3
MOURNFUL   dreorig; reonig; sad
MOUTH   muð (-as) m.
MOVE   glidan 1; hraenan i; lacan 7; strican 1;
    wagian ii; wegan 3
MOVE ABOUT   hweorfan 3
MOVE QUICKLY   bregdan 3; plegan i
MOVE RAPIDLY   stincan 3
MOVEMENT, PLAY OF   lac (-) n.
MOVEMENT, QUICK   braegd (-as) m.; plega (-n) m.
MOVER   -genga (-n) m.
MOW   mawan 7
MUCH OF   fela
MULTIPLY   gemanigfieldan i
MULTITUDE (FORCE AND POWER)   dryht (-a) f.
MULTITUDE (NUMBER)   menigu f.
MURDER   cwalu f.; myrðrung (-a) f.
MURDERER   cwellere (cwelleras) m.
MUSIC   gleo (-) n.
MUSICAL INSTRUMENT   horn (-as) m.

51

N

NAIL   naegl (-as) m.
NAILED   naegled
NAKED   baer; nacod
NAME   nama (-n) m.
NAME   namian ii
NAME (BE CALLED)   hatan 7
NAME, CALL BY   nemnan i
NAP   hnappian ii
NARRATION   racu (raca) f.
NARRATIVE   talu (tala) f.
NARROW (PAINFUL)   enge; nearu
NARROW (PHYSICALLY)   smael
NARROWNESS   engu (enge) f.
NATION   f.
NATIONALS OF   -wara; -waran; -waras; -ware pl.
    suff.
NATURE   gecynd (-a) f.; gecynde (gecyndu) n.
NATURE (BY BIRTH)   byrd (-a) f.; byrdu f.
NATURE (BY FATE)   gescaeft (-a) f.
NAUGHT   naht n.
NEAR   geneahsen a.; neah a. av.
NEAR TO   gehende a.; neah prep.
NEARLY   lytesna
NECESSARY   niedful; ꝺearf
NECESSARILY   niede
NECESSITOUS   ꝺearfende
NECESSITY   nead/nied (-a) f.; ꝺearf (-a) f.
NECK   heals (-as) m.; hnecca (-n) m.; swiera
    (-n) m.
NECKLACE   mene (menas) m.; sigle (siglu) n.
NEED   nead/nied (-a) f.; ꝺearf (-a) f.
NEED   ꝺearfian ii; ꝺurfan prp.
NEEDLE   naedl (-a) f.
NEEDY PERSON   ꝺearfa (-n) m.; waedling (-as) m.
NEGLECT   recceliest f.
NEGLIGENT   saene
NEIGHBORHOOD   neahwist m. f.
NEITHER   ne neg. part.
NEITHER OF TWO   nahwaeꝺer; nawꝺer
NEPHEW   nefa (-n) m.; suhterga m.
NEST   nest (-) n.

NEST   nestlian ii
NET   nett (-) n.
NEVER   na; naefre
NEVERTHELESS   (ge)hwaeðer(e); ðeahna
NEW   niew
NEWLY   niewe
NEXT   aefterra
NEXT TO   birihte
NIGGARDLY   hneaw
NIGHT   niht (-) f.
NIGHT BEFORE   geostran a. av.
NINE   nigun
NINETEEN   niguntiene
NINETY   hundniguntig
NINTH   nigoða
NO   ne av. conj.
NOBILITY   aeðelu f. n. pl.
NOBLE   aeðele; cynerof; freo
NOBLEMAN   aeðeling (-as) m.
NOISE   breaht (-as) m.; cirm (-as) m.; gehlynn
        n.; gestun (-) n.; hleahtor m.; hlemm (-as)
        m.; hlynn n.; prass m.; wom m.; woma (-n)
        m.; woð (-a) f.
NOISE, MAKE A   cierman i; hlydran i
NONE   nan; naenig
NOON   middaeg m.; non f. n.
NO ONE   nan
NOR   ne
NORTH   norð
NORTH, FROM THE   norðan av.
NORTHERN   norðerne
NORTHMOST   norðmest
NOSE   nosu (nosa) f.
NOSTRIL   nosðyrel (-u) n.
NOT   na av.; naht av.; ne neg. part.
NOT AT ALL   na
NOTHING   naht n.
NOURISH   fostrian ii
NOW (THAT)   nu
NOW (THEN)   nuða
NUMBER (TALLY)   talu (tala) f.; tael (talu) n.
NUMBER OF, LARGE   worn (-as) m.
NURTURE   fedan i

O

OAK   ac (aec) m.
OAR   ar (-a) f.
OATH   að (-as) m.; aðswyrd (-) n.
OBEDIENCE   hiersumnes f.
OBEDIENT   hiersum
OBEY   hieran i
OBSERVATION   hield (-a) f.
OBSTACLE   meorring (-a) f.
OCCASION   sael (-e) f.; sið (-as) m.
OCCUPY ONESELF   bisigian ii
OCCURRENCE   gelimp (-u) n.
ODOR   stenc (-as) m.; swaecc (swaccas) m.
OFFENSE   aeswic (-as) m.; aefðanca (-n) m.; inca
    (-n) m.; laeððu f.
OFFER   beodan 2
OFFER SACRIFICE   offrian ii
OFFERING   lac (-u) f.; onsaegednes (-a) f.
OFFICE (FUNCTION)   ambiht (-u) n.
OFFICIAL   gerefa (-n) m.
OFFSPRING   team m.; tudor (-) n.; wocor f.
OFTEN   gelome; geneahhe; oft
OIL   ele m. n.
OINTMENT   nard m.; smeoru (-) n.
OLD   eald; frod; gamol; har
OLD, GROW   ealdian ii
ON   in prep.; on av. prep.
ONE   an a. pro.; aenig a. pro.
ONE (INDEFINITE)   man
ONLY   anga
ONSLAUGHT   raes (-as) m.
ONWARD   forð
OPEN   openian ii; scaenan i
OPEN UP   yppan i
OPEN   open; yppe
OPENING   muð (-as) m.
OPINION   dom (-as) m.; wen (-e) f.
OPPRESS   dreccan i; naetan i; ðraestan i
OPPRESSION   ðroht m.
OR   oððe
ORANGE   read
ORATOR   ðyle (ðylas) m.
ORATORY   gebedhus (-) n.

ORDER (COMMAND)   bebod (-) n.; gebod (-) n.;
    haes (-e) f.; tael (talu) n.
ORDER (COMMAND)   hatan 7; stihtan i
ORDER (REQUEST)   biddan i-6
ORGAN   organan f. pl.
ORIENTAL   easterne; easteweard
ORIGIN   cyme (cyma) f.; frumð/frymð (-as) m.;
    gecynd (-a) f.
ORNAMENT   faet (-) n.; gemm (-as) m.; gleng (-a)
    f.; hyrst (-) f.; wraett (-as) m.
ORNAMENT   gegearwian ii; glengan i
ORNAMENTED   faeted; gewloh
ORPHAN   steopbearn (-) m.; steopcild (ru) n.
OTHER   oðer
OTHERWISE   ellcor; elles
OUT   ut
OUT OF   of
OUTFIT   hyrstan i
OUTLAW   utlaga (-n) m.; wearg (-as) m.
OUTSIDE   ut
OUTSIDE OF   butan
OVEN   ofen (-as) m.
OVER   ofer av. prep.; uppan av. prep.
OVERFLOWING   flede
OWN   stealdan i
OWN, ONE'S   agen; swaes
OWNER   agend (-) m.
OX   oxa (-n) m.
OYSTER   ostre (ostra) f.

P

PACE   feðe n.; -gang (-as) m.
PACIFY   seman i
PAGAN   haeðena (-n) m.
PAGAN   haeðen
PAIN   oncyðð (-a) f.; sar (-) n.; swinc (-as)
    m.; wearc (-) n.; wracu (wraca) f.
PAINFUL   sar; sarig
PAINFULLY   sare
PAIN IN THE ASS   endwerc (-) n.
PALATE   goma (-n) m.
PALE   blacian ii; blatian ii; wanian ii
PALE   blat(e); wan(n)
PALM TREE   palma m.

PAPER (PARCHMENT)   bocfell (-) n.
PARABLE   bispell (-) n.
PARALLEL   efen
PART   dael (-as) m.
PART   syndrian i, ii; twaeman i
PARTAKE OF   ðicgan i-5
PARTAKE OF FOOD   reordian ii
PARTAKING   ðegn (ðega) f.
PARTITION   dal (-) n.; gedal (-) n.
PASS BY   iernan 3
PASS OVER   glidan 1; ofergan anv.
PASS THROUGH   glidan 1; ðurhgan anv.
PASSING (TEMPORARY)   hwilen
PASSION (CHRIST'S SUFFERING)   ðrowung (-a) f.
PASSIONATE   hat; hatwende
PASTURE   edisc (-as) m.
PATERNAL   faederen- pref.
PATH   paeð (paðas) m.
PATH, NARROW   anpaeð (anpaðas) m.
PATH, STEEP   stig (-a) f.
PATIENCE   ðyld (-a) f.
PATIENT   ðyldig
PAY   hyr (-a) f.
PAY   gieldan 3
PAY, WITHOUT   unceapunga
PAYMENT   gield (-) n.
PEACE   freod (-a) f.; friðu (friða) f.; frið m.
     n.; grið n.; liss/lids (-a) f.
PEACE, MAKE   friðian ii
PEACEFUL   som; smolt
PEACEFULLY   smolte
PEACOCK   pea (-n) m.
PEAL   hring (-as) m.
PEARL   meregrota (-n) m.
PEN   penn (-as) m.
PENALTY   steor f.
PENETRATE   feolan 3; stician ii; stingan 3
PENIS   waepen (-) n.
PENNY   pening (-as) m.
PEOPLE   folc (-) n.; fylce n.; ielde m. pl.;
     leode m. pl.; ðeod (-a) f.
PEPPER   pipor m.
PERFORMANCE   plega (-n) m.; weorc (-)' n.
PERHAPS   wenunga
PERISH   breoðan 2; brosnian ii

PERMISSION   leaf (-a) f.; tigð (-a) f.
PERMIT   liefan i; tigðian ii; ðafian ii
PERMITTED TO , BE   motan prp.
PERPETUAL   sin-pref.
PERSECUTE   ehtan i
PERSECUTION   ehtnes (-a) f.; oht (-a) f.; wracu
    (wraca) f.
PERSISTENT   ðrohtig
PERTAINING TO   aetlenge; -lenge; tolenge
PERVERSE   fraete; ðweorh
PETITION   ben (-e) f.
PETITIONER   bena (-n) m.
PHANTOM   scinn n.; scinnan m. pl.
PHYSICIAN   laece (laecas) m.
PICK   ahneopan 2
PICK OUT   lesan 5
PIECE   stycce (styccu) n.
PIERCE   ðurhsmugan 2
PIERCED   ðyrel
PIG   swin (-) n.
PILE UP   hladan 6
PILLAR   stapol (-as) m.
PILOT   steora (-n) m.
PINE AWAY   aswaeman i
PIRATE   lidmann (lidmenn) m.; wicing (-as) m.
PISS   micga (-n) m.; micge (-an) f.
PISS   micgian ? ii?
PISSING   micgung f.
PIT   pytt (-as) m.; seað (-as) m.
PITCH (TAR)   pic m.
PITCHER   crog (-as) m.
PLACE   stael n.; steal (-as) m.; steal (-u) n.;
    stede m.; stow (-a) f.; wang (-as) m.
PLACE   stellan i
PLACE, TAKE   stellian ii
PLAIN   wang (-as) m.
PLAN   ðanc (-as, -u) m. n.; ðeaht (-u) f. n.
PLAN   mamrian ii; sierwan i
PLANK   bord (-) n.; stocc (-as) m.
PLANT   waestm (-as, -a) m. f.; wyrt (-a) f.
PLATE   disc (-as) m.
PLATE-METAL   faet (-) n.
PLAY OF COLOR   brigd m.
PLAY   plegan i
PLEASANT   geryde; hiere; weðe

PLEASE   cweman i; lician ii
PLEASING   cweme
PLEASURE   willa (-n) m.
PLEDGE   að (-as) m.; wedd (-) n.
PLENTY   fyllað m.; fyllu f.
PLENTY OF   genog
PLOT   sierwan i; webbian ii; wrencan i
PLUCK   ahneopan 2
PLUNDER   reaf (-) n.
PLUNDER   beriefan i; hloðian ii; hyðan i; hyðian
    ii; reafian ii; strudan 2
POEM   fitt (-a) f.; giedd (-) n.; gieddung (-a)
    f.; leoð (-) n.; sang (-as) m.
POET   scop (-as) m.
POINT   brerd (-as) m.; gad f.; ord (-) n.
POINT THE WAY   wisian ii
POISON   ator (-) n.
POISONOUS   aetren
POLISH   biewan i; feormian ii; sweorfan 3
POLISHER   biewend (-) m.; feormend (-) m.
POLLUTE   widlian ii
POMMEL   hilt (-as) m.
POND   mere m.
PONDER   ðeahtian ii
POOR   earm; waedle
POOR IN   orfierme
POOR MAN   unaga (-n) m.; waedling (-as) m.
POPE   papa (-n) m.
PORCH   portic m.
PORTAL   dor (-u) n.
PORTION   dael (-as) m.; gemet (-u) n.
POSITION (MILITARY)   stede m.
POSSESS   agan prp.; stealdan i
POSSESSION   bearm (-as) m.; feorm (-a) f.
POSSESSIONS   aeht (-e) f.
POSSIBLY   wenunga
POT   hwer (-as) m.
POTENT   craeftig
POUND   brysan i; cnossian ii
POUR   geotan 2
POUR A DRINK   byrelian ii; scencan i
POVERTY   iermðu (iermða) f.; waedl f.
POWER   afol n.; craeft (-) n.; eafoð (eafoðu)
    n.; maegen (-) n.; meaht (-a) f.; weald f.
    n. ; wield (-) n.

POWERFUL   craeftig; mihtig; ðryðig
PRAISE   herenes (-a) f.; lof m. n.
PRAISE   herian i; lofian ii; weorðian ii
PRAY   biddan i-5
PRAYER   bed (-u) n.
PREACH   bodian ii
PRECIPITOUS   neowol; stealc
PREFIXES: SEE LIST
PREGNANT, BECOME   eacnian ii
PREGNANT   eacen
PREOCCUPATION   bisigu (bisiga) f.
PREPARE   bierwan i; gearwan i; gearwian ii; reg-
    nian ii; reordian ii; teo(ga)n ii
PRESCRIBE   scrifan 1
PRESENCE   midwist m. f.
PRESENT   iewan i
PRESENT   andweard
PRESERVATION   hield (-a) f.
PRESS   crudan 2; ðringan 3; ðywan i
PRESS ON   tingan 3
PRESS UPON   ðryccan i
PRESSING   ðrohtig
PRESSURE   geðring n.
PREVENT   dwellan i; lettan i
PRICE   ceap (-as) m.; weorð n.
PRIDE   bielc m.; gaelsa (-n) m.; gemetu (gemet-
    ta) f.; gielp m. n.; medla m.; wlencu (wlen-
    ca) f.
PRIEST   maessere (maesseras) m.; preost (-as) m.;
    sacerd (-as) m.
PRINCE   aeðeling (-as) m.; fengel (fenglas) m.;
    leod m.; raeswa (-n) m.; ðeoden (ðeodnas) n.;
    ðengel (ðenglas) m.
PRISON   carcaern n.; cweartaern n.; dung (dyng)
    f.; faesten (-) n.; loc (-u) n.; loca (-n) m.
PRISONER   haefta (-n) m.; haeftling (-as) m.
PRISONER, BOUND   raepling (-as) m.
PRISONER, TAKE   haeftnian ii
PRIVY   gangpitt (-as) m.; utgang (-as) m.
PROCEED   drifan 1; wadan 6
PROCLAIM   bannan 7; meldan i; meldian ii
PROCLAMATION   bann (-) n.; meld (-a) f.
PROD   bryrdan i
PRODUCE (PROGENY)   tydran i
PRODUCTIVE   forðbaere

PRODUCTIVITY   forðbaeru f.
PROFIT   nyttung (-a) f.
PROGENY   tudor (-) n.; wocor f.
PROMISE   beot (-) n.
PROMISE   andettan i; hatan 7
PROMOTE   stiepan i
PROP   wraðu f.
PROP UP   wreðian ii
PROPER   gemet; riht
PROPERTY   aeht (-e) f.; feoh (-) n.
PROPHECY   witegdom (-as) m.
PROPHESY   witegian ii
PROPHET   witga (-n) m.
PROSPER   spowan 7; spedan i; ðeon 1, 3; weligian
    ii.
PROSPERITY   blaed (-as) m.; sael (-e) m. f.;
    saelð (-a) f.; sped (-e) f.
PROSPEROUS   saelig; spedig; (ge)ðungen; welig
PROSTRATE   streccan i
PROTECT   beorgan 3; hedan i; scieldan i; sparian
    ii
PROTECTION   eodor (-as) m.; faeðm (-as) m.; helm
    (-as) m.; hield n.; hleow m.; hreoða (-n) m.;
    mund (-a) f.; scield (-as) m.; waru (wara)
    f.; waer f.
PROTECTOR   eodor (-as) m.; friða (-n) m.; gehola
    (-n) m.; helm (-as) m.; hleow m.
PROUD, BE   modigan ii; ðunian ii
PROUD   deall; fraete; fraetig; modig; wlanc
PROW   heals (-as) m.
PRUDENT   snotor
PSALM   sealm (-as) m.; sealma (-n) m.
PSALMS, SING   sealmettan ii
PUBLICAN   taeppere (taepperas) m.
PULL   teon 2; togian ii
PUNISH   witnian ii
PUNISHMENT   wite (-) n.
PUPIL   leornere (leorneras) m.
PUPPY   hwelp (-as) m.
PURE   bilewit; claene; hlutor; smaete
PURIFY   claensian ii; faelsian ii; hlutrian ii;
    merian i
PURPLE   haewen
PURPLE DYE   wurma (-n) m.
PURPLE PERIWINKLE   wurma (-n) m.

PURPOSE   forsetenes (-a) f.
PURSUIT OF, IN   onlast(e) prep.
PUSH   scufan 2
PUT   stellan i
PUT ON (OR OFF)   sliepan i
PYRE   ad (-as) m.
PYRE, FUNERAL   bael n.

Q

QUAKE   cwacian ii
QUEEN   cwen (-e) f.
QUARTERS, SLEEPING   bur (-as) m.
QUESTION   frasung (-a) f.; fraegn m. n.
QUICK   hraed- pref.; hwaet; (h)raeđ; recen; snell
    snud
QUICKEN   cwician ii
QUICKLY   aedre; ellne; (h)raeđe; recene; sneome;
    snude
QUICK-WITTED   scearp
QUIET   row (-a) f.
QUIET, GROW   sessian ii; stillan i
QUIET   still
QUIETLY   stille

R

RACE (NATIONALITY)   byrdu f.; cynn (-) n.
RADIANCE   scima (-n) m.
RADIANT   glaed
RAFT   fleot (-as) m.
RAGE   grimman 3; hwelan 4; styrman i; wedan i;
    ystan i
RAGING   wod
RAID   hergian ii
RAIN   regn (-as) m.
RAIN   regnian ii
RAINY   regnig
RAISE   hebban i-6; raeran i
RAM (ANIMAL)   ramm (-as) m.
RAMPART   weall (-as) m.
RAPE   reafian ii
RARE   aenlic; seld- pref.
RARELY   seldan av.
RASP   feol (-a) f.

RATTLE   hrissan i
RAVAGE   reafian ii
RAVEN   hraefn (-as) m.
RAW   hreaw
REACH   raecan i
READ   raedan 7-i
READILY   gear(w)e av.
READY   gearwian ii; gierwan i; redian ii
READY   gearu; geryde
REALM   rice (ricu) n.
REAP   ripan 1
REAPER   riftere (rifteras) m.
REASON   wis (-e) f.
REASONABLY   scadlice
REBUKE   hosp (-as) m.
REBUKE   ðreagan ii
RECALL   myndigian ii
RECEIVE   ðecgan i; ðicgan i-5
RECEIVER   tigða (-n) m.
RECEIVING   ðegu (ðega) f.
RECEPTACLE   faetels m.
RECITE   wrecan 5
RECITE A LAY   gieddian ii
RECITE POETRY   singan 3
RECKON   tellan i
RECLINING   hlin- pref.
RECOGNIZE   cnawan 7
RECONCILIATION   grið n.; sibb (-a) f.
RECOVER   wierpan i
RED   read; reod
REDISH-BROWN, GLOSSY   brunbasu
RED-PURPLE   basu
REDDEN   reodan 2
REDEEM   abycgan i
REDEEMER   aliesend (-) m.
REDEMPTION   liesnes (-a) f.
REFINED   smaete
REFLECT UPON   smeagan i
REFUGEE   fliema (-n) m.; wrecca (-n) m.
REFUSAL   wearn (-a) f.
REFUSE   wiernan i
REFUSE OBEDIENCE TO   forhylman i
REGARD FOR   myne (-) m.
REGENERATE   bredian ii
REGENERATION   edscaeft f.

REGRET   gehreowan 7; hreowan 7; murnan 3
REGULATE   stefnan i
REJOICE   drieman i; faegnian ii; feon 5; gielpan
    3; gladrian ii; gliewan ii
REJOICING   blissung (-a) f.; feowung (-a) f.
RELATE   bodian ii
RELATIVE   gaedeling (-as) m.
RELATIVES   cnosl n.
RELEASE   liesan i
RELIABILITY   treow (-a) f.
RELIGION   aefaestnes (-a) f.
RELISH   sufel (-) n.
RELISHES, PROVIDE WITH   syflan i
REMAIN   wunian ii
REMARKABLE   seld- pref.
REMEDY   bot (-a) f.
REMEMBER   munan prp.
REMISS, BECOME   seolcan 3
REMOVE   forpyndan i
REMOVE TO AFAR   fierran i
REND   rendan i
REPAY   gieldan 3
REPENT   behreosian ii
REPENTANT   hreow
REPLY   andcwiss (-a) f.
REPORTER   melda (-n) m.
REPOSE   restan i
REPROACH   edwit (-) n.; hosp (-as) m.; tael f.
REPROACH   taelan i
REPTILE   wyrm (-as) m.
REPUTE   hlisa m.
REQUIRE   behofian ii; frasian ii
RESCUE   hreddan i
RESIDENCE   set (-u) n.
RESIDENTS OF   -waran; -waras; -ware; -waru pl.
    suff.
RESIDUE   laf (-as) m.
RESOUND   hleoðrian ii; hlimman 3; hlynnan i;
    hlynsian ii; scralletan i; swogan 7
RESPECT   arian ii
REST   raest (-a) f.; row (-a) f.
REST   restan i
RESTING PLACE   raest (-a) f.; stre(o)wen
    (streona) f.
RESTORE   bredian ii

RESTRAINT, SELF   forhaefednes f.; onbaeru f.
RESTRICTED   nearu
RESTRICTEDLY   nearwe
RESURRECTION   aerist   m. f. n.
RETAINER   gesið (-as) m.
RETAINERS   folgere (folgeras) m.
RETAINERS, BAND OF   dryht (-a) f.
RETINUE   folgað (-as) m.
RETREAT   bugan 2
REVEAL   sweotolian ii
REVELRY, NOISY   gleam m. n.
REVENGE   faehð(u) (faehða) f.; wraec (-u) n.
REVENGE   wrecan 5
REVOLVE   hwearfian ii; swifan 1
REWARD   lean (-) n.; med (-a) f.; meord (-a) f.
REWARD   leanian ii
RIB   ribb (-) n.
RICH   rice
RIDDLE   raedelle (raedellan) f.
RIDE   ridan 1
RIDING   rad (-a) f.
RIGHT   ae f.; riht (-) n.
RIGHT   riht a.
RIGHTEOUS   rihtwis
RIGHTLY   rihte av.
RIM   rand (-as) m.
RIME   hrim m.
RIND   rind (-a) f.
RING   beag (-as) m.; hring (-as) m.; wriða (-n)
    m.
RING OUT   hringan 3; neomian ii
RINSE   swillan i; swillian ii
RIP   teran 4
RISE   risan 1; stincan 3
RISK   neðan i
ROAM   waeðan i
ROAR   brastelian ii; grymettan i; hrutan 2;
    hwelan 4; stunian ii
ROB   beriefan i; hlyðan i; reofan 2
ROBBER   reafere (reaferas) m.
ROCK   carr (-as) m.
ROCKS, MASS OF   clud (-as) m.
ROD   gierd f.; lael (-a) f.
ROLL   trendlian ii; wealcan 7; wealwian ii;
    worian ii

ROLLING (OF WAVES)   gewealc (-) n.
ROOF   hrof (-as) m.; ðaca (-n) m.; ðaec (ðacu) n.
ROOF   hrefan i
ROOM   bur (-as) m.
ROOMY   rum; wid
ROOT   stefn (-as) m.; stefna (-n) m.; truma (-n)
    m.
ROOT OUT   awyrtwalian ii
ROOT UP   wrotan 7
ROPE   rap (-as) m.; sal (-as) m.
ROSE   rose (rosan) f.
ROUGH   hreof; hreoh; ruh
ROUSE   hwettan i
ROUT   flieman i
ROUTE   paeð (paðas) m.; weg (-as) m.
ROW   rowan 7
ROWER   rowend (-) m.
ROYAL   cyne- pref.; cynelic
RUB   sweorfan 3
RUDDY   reod
RUIN   spild m.
RUINS, IN   hreorig
RULE   gemet (-u) n.; regol (-as) m.
RULE   agan prp.; healdan 7; racian ii; raedan
    7-i; ricsian ii; wealdan 7; wieldan i
RULER   agend (-) m.; brego m.; raedend (-) m.;
    stihtend (-as) m.; ðengel (ðenglas) m.; weal-
    dend (-) m.; wealda (-n) m.
RUN   hleapan 7; iernan 3; ðraegan i
RUNG   hrung (-a) f.
RUSE   wrenc (-as) m.
RUSH   raes (-as) m.
RUSH (WATER)   geotan 2
RUSH, MAKE A   raesan i
RUST   om m.
RUSTY   omig

S

SACRAMENT   husl (-) n.
SACRIFICE   blot (-) n.; lac (-) f. n.; onsaeged-
    nes (-a) f.; tiber/tifer (-) n.
SACRIFICE   blotan 7
SACRIFICE, OFFER   tifrian ii
SACRIFICIAL OFFERING   tiber/tifer (-) n.

SAD   geomor; reonig; reotig; sarig
SAD, BE   dreorigian ii
SADDLE   sadol (-as) m.
SAFETY   ner (-) n.; sundfulnes (-a) f.
SAIL   segl (-as) m.
SAIL   lidan i; siglan i; swimman 3
SAILOR   ferend (-) m.; flota (-n) m.; lida (-) m.
SAINT   halig (-e) m.; sanct (-as) m.
SAINTED   sanct
SALMON   leax (-as) m.
SALMON, SPAWNING   cypera (-n) m.
SALT   sealt n.
SALTY   sealt
SALTWATER   sealt n.
SALUTARY   halwende; sundful
SALUTE   gretan i; haelsian ii
SALVATION   hals f.; hael (-) n.; haelu f.
SAME   ilca
SAME, THE   se ilca
SAME WAY, IN THE   same
SAND   sand (-) n.
SAP   saep m.; wos n.
SATED, BE   sadian ii
SATED WITH   saed
SATURDAY   Saeterndaeg (Saeterndagas) m.
SAVE   hreddan i; nerian i
SAVIOR   geocend m.; haelend m.; neriend m.
SAY   cwedan 5; secgan i; sciran i
SAYING   cwide (-) n.; gieddung (-a) f.; saegen
    (-a) f.
SCALP   haettian ii
SCATTER   sprengan i; stregdan 3
SCATTER ABOUT   stencan i; swengan i
SCHOLAR   bocere (boceras) m.; udwita (-n) m.
SCORN   bismer m. f. n.; husc (-as) m.
SCORN   aewan i; bismerian ii; hyspan i
SCOUR   feormian ii
SCOURGE   swingan 3; swipan ii
SCOURGER   swingere (swingeras) m.
SCRATCH   writan 1
SCREAM   hream (-as) m.
SCREAM   giellan 3
SCRIBE   writere (writeras) m.
SCRIPTURE   writ (-u) n.
SEA   brim (-u) n.; ear (-as) m.; flod (-as) m.;

SEA (CONTD.)   flot n.; garsecg m.; geofon n.;
    haef (hafu) n.; haern (-a) f.; holm (-as)
    m.; lagu m.; mere m.; rad (-a) f.; seoloð
    (-as) m.; waed (wadu) n.
SEA-COAST   brim (-u) n.; ende (endas) m.
SEAGULL   maew (-as) m.
SEA-MONSTER   fifel (-) n.; nicor (-as) m.
SEAL (ANIMAL)   seolh (seolas) m.
SEAT   set (-u) n.; setl (-) n.; sess (-as) m.;
    stol (-as) m.
SEAWEED   war (-) n.
SEAWEED, COVERED WITH   warig
SECOND   aefterra; oðer
SECRET   run (-a) f.; ryne (rynu) n.
SECRET, KEEP   diernan i
SECRET   dierne; onhaele
SECRETLY   diegle
SECURE   faestnian ii
SECURE   trum
SECURITY   faestnung (-a) f.; frið m. n.; friðu
    (friða) f.
SEE   gewitan i; seon 5
SEED   cið (-as) m.; saed (-) n.
SEEK   secan i
SEEM   ðyncan i
SEIZE   fon 7; grapian ii
SEIZING   aetgraepe a.
SELECT   ceosan 2; lesan 5
SELF   self
SELL   bebycgan i
SEND   sendan i
SENSIBLE   wittig
SENTENCE   scrifan 1
SEPARATE   feorrsian ii; sundrian ii; syndran i;
    syndrian ii; twaeman i
SEPARATE   syndrig
SEPARATION   dal (-) n.; gedal (-) n.
SERAPHIM   seraphin
SERENE   smylte
SERIOUS   gestaeððig
SERIOUSLY   sare
SERPENT   naedre (naedran) f.; wyrm (-as) m.
SERVANT   esne (esnas) m.; scealc (-as) m.; ðeow
    (-as) m.
SERVE   ðegnian ii; ðeowian ii

SERVICE   bryce m.; ðegnung (-a) f.; ðeowot (-u) n.
SET   settan i
SETTLE   buan 7-iii
SETTLEMENT   bu- pref.; wic (-) n.
SEVEN   seofun
SEVENFOLD   seofunfeald
SEVENTEEN   seofuntiene
SEVENTH   seofoða
SEVENTY   seofuntig
SEVERE   enge; geocor; hefig; hreoh; strang; ðearl
SEVERELY   stiernunga; ðearle
SEW   seowan i; seowian ii
SHACKLE   scaecel (-as) m.
SHADE   scadu (scadwa) f.; scaed (scadu) n.; scu(w)a (-n) m.
SHADOW   scadu (scadwa) f.; scaed (scadu) n.
SHAFT (OF A SPEAR)   scaeft (-as) m.
SHAKE   cweccan i; hrissan i; wagian ii
SHAKING   wancol
SHAKY   tealt
SHALL   sculan prp.
SHAME   aewisc f.; orwierðu f.; scamu (scama) f.; scand (-a) f.
SHAME   scendan i
SHANK   scanca (-n) m.
SHARE   dael (-as) m.; hliet (-as) m.
SHARE   daelan i
SHARP   biter; hwaet; scearp; sticol
SHARPEN   scierpan i
SHARPLY   bitere
SHATTER   scaenan i
SHEAF (OF GRAIN)   sceaf (-as) m.
SHEAR   scieran 4
SHEATH (SWORD)   scaeð (-a) f.
SHEDDING (BLOOD)   gyte m.
SHEEP   sceap (-) n.
SHELF   scielfe (scielfa) f.
SHELL   sciell (-a) f.
SHEPHERD   sceaphierde (sceaphierdas) m.
SHERIFF   gerefa (-n) m.
SHIELD   bord (-) n.; rand (-as) m.; scield (-as) m.
SHIELD, LINDEN   lind (-a) f.

SHIELD   scieldan i
SHIFTING   waefre
SHILLING   scilling (-as) m.
SHINE   blican 1; leohtian ii; liexan i; scimian
     ii; scinan i; tytan i
SHINE, CAUSE TO   scaenan ii
SHIP   ceol (-as) m.; cnear (-as) m.; flota (-n)
     m.; lid (-u) n.; naca (-n) m.; scip (-u) n.;
     scrad (-a) f.
SHIP, HIGH-PROWED   brenting (-as) m.
SHIT   scitte f.
SHIT   bescitan 1
SHOD (OF HORSES)   calcrand
SHOES, PAIR OF   scy n. pl.
SHOOT   sceotan 2; scotian ii
SHOOT INTO   sceotan 2
SHOOT FORWARD   sceotan 2
SHORE   brim (-u) n.; staeð (-as) m.
SHORT   scort
SHORTEN   scyrtan i
SHOT   gescot (-u) n.; scur (-as) m.; scyte m.
SHOULDER   bod (-as) m.; eaxl (-a) f.
SHOULDERS   gesculdre/gescyldre f. pl.
SHOVE   scufan 2
SHOW   iewan i
SHOWER OF WEAPONS   scur (-as) m.
SHRINK   scrincan 3
SHRINK DOWN INTO   clingan 3
SHRIVEL   forwisnian ii
SHUN   scunian ii
SHUNNED, BE   scuniendlic
SHUT   clysan i
SHUT IN   heaðorian ii
SHUT THE EYES   wincian ii
SHUT UP   clemman i
SHY   bleað
SICK   seoc
SICKLY   coðlice
SICKNESS   wol m.
SIDE   healf (-a) f.
SIDE OF A SHIP   bord (-) n.
SIGH   sicettung (-a) f.
SIGHT   sihð f.; sien f.
SIGN   beacen (-n) n.; biecð (-a) f.; segn (-) n.;
     tacen (-) n.

69

SIGN, MAKE A   beacnian ii; tacnian ii
SILENCE   row f.; swige f.
SILENT, BECOME   swigian ii
SILENT   still; swige
SILENTLY   stille
SILK   seoluc (-as) m.
SILLY   dwol a. pref.
SILVER   seolfor n.
SILVER   seolfren
SIMILAR   gelic
SIMILARITY   gelic n.
SIMPLE   anfeald; unorne
SIMULATE   licettan i
SIN   synn (-a) f.
SIN   gyltan i; synnigian ii
SINCE   siđđan
SINEW   seonu (seonwa) f.
SINFUL   synnig
SING   galan 6; singan 3
SING A SONG   leođian ii
SINGER   sangere (sangeras) m.
SINGER OF TALES   scop (-as) m.
SINGLE   syndrig
SINK   sigan 1; sincan 3
SINK, CAUSE TO   saegan i; sencan i
SINK TO THE GROUND   gryndan i
SIP   supan 2
SISTER   sweostor (-) f.; gesweostor f. pl.
SIT   sittan i
SIX   siex
SIXTH   siexta
SIXTY   siextig
SIZE   micelnes (-a) f.
SKILL   orđanc m.; searu (-) n.
SKINN   scinn (-u) n.; sweard (-as) m.
SKY   heofon (-as) m.; rodor (-as) m.; swegel n.
SLACK, BECOME   seolcan 3
SLACK   sleac
SLAUGHTER   wael (walu) n.
SLAVE   đeow (-as) m.
SLAY   slean 6; swebban i
SLAYER   bana (-n) m.; slaga (-n) m.
SLEEP   slaep m.; swefn (-) n.; swefot n.
SLEEP   slaepan 7; swefan 5
SLEEP, PUT TO   swebban i

SLEET   hagol/haegel (haeglas) m. n.
SLENDER   swancor; ðynne
SLICE   snaed (-as) m.
SLIDE   slidan 1
SLIGHT   maete; ðynne
SLIP   slide (slidas) m.
SLIP   slidan 1; sliepan i
SLIP AWAY   slupan 2
SLIPPERY   slidor
SLIT   slitan 1
SLOPE   hlið (-u, -) n.
SLOPE   hieldan i; hlinian ii
SLOPING   -heald suff.
SLOTH   oferslaep m.
SLOTHFUL   slaw
SLOW   laet; saene; slaw; sleac
SLOW UP   lettan i
SLUMBER   sluma m.
SMALL   lytel; medeme; smael
SMALL (AMOUNT)   lyt n. a. av.
SMEAR   smierwan i; smitan 1
SMITH   smið (-as) m.
SMOKE   riec (-as) m.; ðrosm (-as) m.
SMOKE   reocan 2; riecan i
SMOOTH   smeðe
SNAIL   snaegl (-as) m.
SNAKE   naedre (naedran) f.; wyrm (-as) m.
SNARE   grin f. n.; hinderhoc m.; sada (-n) m.
SNOW   snaw (-as) m.
SNOW   sniwan i
SO   swa; ðus
SOAK   wesan i
SOAKING   sype m.
SOB   geoxa (-n) m.
SOB   geocsian ii
SOCIETY   gaed n.
SOFT   hnesce; mearu
SOFTEN   ðweran 4
SOFTLY   sefte/softe
SOIL   fold (-an) f.
SOIL   smitan 1
SOLE   anga; anlic
SOLID   heard; stið
SOLITARY   anlic; anliepe
SOLITARY ONE   anstapa (-n) m.

71

SOLLAR   solor (-as) m.
SOMEONE   hwa; hwaet
SOMEWHAT   hwaene av.
SON   byre (byras, -) m.; maga (-n) m.; magu (ma-
    ga) m.; maeg (-as) m.; maega (-n) m.; sunu
    (suna) m.
SONG   fitt (-a) f.; gealdor (gealdru) n.; gied-
    dung (-a) f.; leoð (-) n.; sang (-as) m.
SOON   hraðor; hraedlic
SOONER   aer; hroðor
SORROW   brecða (-n) m.; gnorn (-as) m.; gnyrn
    (-a) f.; gryn (-as, -) m. n.; hreow (-a) f.;
    sorg (-a) f.
SORROW   sorgian ii
SORROWFUL   hreow
SOUL   sawol (sawla) f.
SOUND   hlemm (-as) m.; hleoðor (-) n.; hring
    (-as) m.; sweg (-as) m.; swinn m.
SOUND   hringan 3; neomian ii; swogan 7; weman i
SOUND CLEARLY   beorhtian ii
SOUND MELODIOUSLY   swinsian ii
SOUND NOISILY   hlemman i
SOUND OUT   heortian ii; hleoðrian ii
SOUTH   suð
SOUTH, DIRECTED TOWARDS THE   suðweardes av.
SOUTH, FROM THE   suðan
SOUTH, INCLINING TOWARD THE   suðheald
SOUTHERN   suð; suðerne; suðheald
SOW   sawan 7
SPACE   rum(a) m. n.
SPACIOUS   geap; ginn; rum
SPADE   spadu (spada) f.
SPARE   sparian ii
SPARK   spearca (-n) n.; ysle (yslan) f.
SPARK   spearcian ii
SPARROW   sperwa (-n) m.
SPEAK   gieddian ii; hleoðrian ii; maðelian ii;
    maeðlan i; maelan i; reordian ii; sprecan 5
SPEAKER   spreca (-n) m.
SPEAR   daroð (-as) m.; gar (-as) m.; spere
    (speru) n.
SPEAR, ASHWOOD   aesc (-as) m.
SPEAR, FRANKISH   franca (-n) m.
SPECTACLE   sceawung (-a) f.; wafung (-a) f.
SPECTRE   scinn n.; scinnan m. pl.

SPEECH   maeðel (-u) n.; reord (-a) f.; spraec
    (-a) f.; talu (tala) f.
SPEECH, FACULTY OF   gesprec (-) n.
SPEECH, OF   -spraece suff.
SPEECHLESS   dumb
SPEED   scyndan i
SPELL   gealdor (gealdru) n.
SPIRIT   blaed (-as) m.; ferhð (-as, -) m. n.;
    feorh (feoras, -) m. n.; gast/gaest (-as) m.
SPIRIT, EVIL   scinn n.; scinnan m. pl.; scucca
    (-n) m.
SPIRITED   modig
SPIT   spaetan i; spiwan 1
SPITTLE   spatl (-) n.
SPLENDID   betlic
SPLENDOR   leoma (-n) m.
SPLIT   cleofan 2; splatan 7
SPOKE   hrung (-a) f.
SPOKEN   -wyrde suff.
SPOKESMAN   ðyle m.
SPORT   gamen n.; plega (-n) m.
SPOT   splott (-as) m.; wamm (-as, -) m. n.
SPOT   wemman i
SPOUSE   gemaecca (-n) m.
SPREAD   sufl n.
SPREADS, PROVIDE WITH   syflan i
SPREAD ABROAD   braedan i
SPREAD OUT   braedan i
SPRING (SEASON)   lencten (-as) m.
SPRING (WATER)   seað (-as) m.; spring/spryng
    (-as) m.; wiell (-as) m.; wiella (-n) m.;
    wielle (wiellan) f.
SPRING   springan 3
SPRING UP   laecan i
SPRINGTIME   lencten (-as) m.
SPRINKLE   leccan i
SPROUT   sprutan 2; sprytan i; spryttan i
STAB   stician ii; stingan 3
STAFF   gierd f.; staef (stafas) m.
STAG   heorot (-as) m.
STAID   gestaeððig
STAIN   wamm (-as, -) m. n.
STAINED   fag
STALK   scriðan 1
STALLION   hengest (-as) m.

STAND   standan 6
STAND BY   laestan i
STAR   steorra (-n) m.; tungol (tunglas, -) m. n.
STAR, MORNING   forerynel (-as) m.
STARE AT   starian ii
STATE (CONDITION)   had (-as) m.
STATEMENT   spell (-) n.
STATION   till (-) n.
STEAD   stael n.
STEALING   stalu f.
STEED   eoh m.; hengest (-as) m.; mearh (mearas)
     m.; wicg (-) n.
STEEL   stiele n.
STEEL, OF   stieled; stielen
STEEP   neowol; staegel; stealc; steap
STEER   stieran i
STEERING   steor (-a) f.
STEM   stefn (-as) m.; stefna (-n) m.; stofn m. n.
STEP   steppan i-6; tredan 5; treddan i; treddian
     ii
STEP-CHILD   steopcild (-ru) n.
STERN   stierne; stið
STICK   sagol (-as) m.
STICK   clifan 1
STICKY   clibbor
STILL   stillan i
STILL (YET)   gegn; gen; giet
STINGY   gneað
STINK   stincan 3
STIPULATION   araednes (-a) f.
STIR   hreran i; styrian i
STIR UP   wregan i
STIRRED, BE   wiellan i
STONE   stan (-as) m.
STONE, OF   staenen
STOP   blinnan 3
STOP UP   dyttan i
STORM   storm (-as) m.; weder (-) n.; yst (-a) f.
STORM, SNOW   hrið (-a) f.
STORM   styrman i; ystan i
STORM-BEATEN   hriðig
STORMY   hreoh; ystig
STORY   sagu (saga) f.; spell (-) n.
STRAIGHT   riht
STRAIGHTEN   rihtan i

STRAP   lael (-a) f.
STRAW   healm (-as) m.; streaw (-) n.
STREAM   broc (-as) m.; rið (-as) m.; stream (-as)
    m.; waeter (-) n.
STREET   straet (-a) f.; weg (-as) m.
STRENGTH   craeft (-) n.; eafoð (-u) n.; ellen n.;
    strengðu f.; strengu (strenge) f.; ðryð (-e)
    f.
STRENGTH, GAIN   maegenian ii
STRENGTHEN   strangian ii; swiðan i; trymian i
STRETCH   streccan i; ðenian i
STRETCHED OUT, BE   ðunian ii
STRIDE   scriðan 1; stridan 1
STRIDING   scride- pref.
STRIFE   sacu (saca) f.; saecc (-a) f.; strið
    (-as) m.; wroht (-a) f.
STRIKE   beatan 7; cnyssan i; drepan 5; hnossian
    ii; slean 6
STRIKE DOWN   bredwian ii
STRING   streng (-as) m.
STRING, HARP   sner (-e) f.
STRIVE   sinnan 3; strutian ii
STRIVE FOR   tilian ii
STROKE   dynt (-as) m.; slege (slegas) m.; sin-
    eng (-as) m.; sweng (-as) m.
STRONG   braesne; bresne; dyhtig; geocor; hror;
    stearc; stierced; strang; swið; ðryðig
STRONGLY   wraeste
STRONG, MAKE   strangian ii
STRONGHOLD   burg (burig) f.; faesten (-) m.
STRUGGLE   gewinn (-) n.
STRUGGLE   sacan 6; winnan 3
STUD   naegl (-as) m.
STUDDED   naegled
STUDY   leornian ii
STUMBLE   tealtrian ii
STUPID   dwaes; medwis
SUBDUE   lissan i
SUBSISTENCE   wist (-a) f.
SUCCEED   spedan i
SUCCESS   sped (-e) f.
SUCCESSFUL   spedig
SUCCESSFULLY   spowendlic(e)
SUCCESSOR   ierfnuma (-n) m.
SUCH   swilc

SUCK   sucan 2; sugan 2
SUDDENLY   faeringa; hraedlice
SUFFIXES: SEE LIST
SUITABLE, BE   byrian i; dafenian ii; risan 1
SUITABLE   dafen; gedefe; gemaec; getaese; risne
SUFFER   dreogan 2; sargian ii; drowian ii
SUFFERER   drowere (droweras) m.
SUFFERING   drowung (-a) f.
SUFFICIENCY   genyht f. n.
SUFFICIENT   genog
SUFFOCATE   drysman i
SULPHUR   swefel m.
SUMMER   sumor (-as) m.
SUMMER SEASON   missere (misseru) n.
SUMMON   langian ii
SUN   segel(e) n.; sunne (sunnan) f.; swegel n.
SUN, RISING   earendel m.
SUNDAY   Sunnandaeg (Sunnandagas) m.
SUPPLIANT   bena (-n) m.
SUPPLICATION   halsung (-a) f.
SUPPORT   andwist (-a) f.; help (-as, -a) m. f.;
    lad (-a, -) f. n.; wradu f.
SUPPORT   swidan i; wredian ii
SUPPOSE   wenan i
SURETY   wedd (-) n.
SURFACE OF THE EARTH   sceat (-as) m.
SURGE   wielm (-as) m.
SURGE OF THE SEA   geswing (-) n.
SURGE   wealcan 7; weallan 7
SURGING   hopig
SURROUND   faedman i; faedmian ii; ymbgan anv.
SURVIVE   diegan i; nesan 5
SUSTAIN   wredian ii
SUSTENANCE   andleofa (-n) m.; feorm (-a) f.;
    fostor m.
SWALLOW   supan 2; swelgan 3
SWAMP   merisc (-as) m.
SWAN   ilfetu (ilfeta) f.; swan (-as) m.
SWEAR   swerian i-6/4
SWEAT   swat m.
SWEAT   swaetan i
SWEATY   swatig
SWEEP   swapan 7
SWEET   swete
SWEETLY   swote

SWELL   bierman i; swellan 3; ðindan 3; ðrindan/
    ðrintan 3
SWELLING   swellung (-a) f.
SWIFT   arod; scrid; swift
SWIM   fleotan 2; swimman 3
SWIMMING   sund n.
SWIMMING, SKILLED IN   syndig
SWINE   swin (-) n.
SWING ONESELF   swingan 3
SWISHING   sumsendre
SWOLLEN-NECKED   belcedsweora
SWOON   swima m.
SWORD   bill (-) n.; brand (-as) m.; iren/isen/
    isern (-) n.; mece (mecas) m.; sweord (-) n.
SWORD, SHORT   seax (-) n.
SYNOD   seonað (-as) m.

T

TABLE   tabule (tabulan) f.
TAIL   finta (-n) m.; steort (-as) m.; taegel
    (-as) m.
TAKE   nimman 4
TAKE ONESELF   medan i
TALE   sagu (saga) f.; saegen (-a) f.
TALL   great; lang
TALKATIVE   cwedol; spraecful
TAMBORINE   timpana (-n) m.
TAME   temian ii
TAME   tam
TAMENESS   tama (-n) m.
TAPER   tapor (-as) m.
TAPESTRY   webb (-) n.
TAR   pic m.
TARGET   miercels m. f.
TASTE   biergan i
TASTELESSNESS   aemelnes (-a) f.
TAVERN-KEEPER   taeppere (taepperas) m.
TAX   gafol n.; gambe (gamban) f.
TEACH   reccan i; seppan i; taecan i
TEACHER   lareow (-as) m.; magister (magistras)
    m.
TEACHING   lar (-a) f.
TEAR (DROP)   tear (-as) m.
TEAR   taesan i; teran 4

TEAR APART   rendan i
TEARFUL   reotig
TEMPER   stielan i
TEMPEST   scur (-as) m.
TEMPLE   tempel (-) n.
TEMPLE (PAGAN)   ealh (-as) m.; hearg (-as) m.
TEMPORAL   hwilwende
TEMPORARY   laene
TEMPT   costian ii; cunnian ii
TEMPTATION   cost(n)ung (-a) f.; cunnung (-a) f.
TEN   tien
TENDER   hnesce; mearu
TENT   traef (trafu) n.
TEPID   wlacu
TERN   stearn (-as) m.
TERRIBLE   egesig; ondrysne
TERRIFY   bregan i; egesian ii; fyrhtan i
TERRIFYING   egesig
TERROR   broga (-n) m.; ege m.; egesa (-n) m.;
    gryre (gryras, -) m.
TESTAMENT   gecyðnes (-a) f.
TESTIFY   seðan i
THANE   ðegn (-as) m.
THAT   ðaet conj.
THATCH   ðecen f.
THATCH   ðeccan i
THAW   ðawian ii
THEN   ðan; ðanne
THEN   ða av. conj.
THENCE   ðanan
THERE   ðaer; ðider
THERE, FROM   ðanan
THICK   ðicce
THIEF   ðeof (-as) m.; reafere (reaferas) m.
THIEVERY   stalu f.
THIN   ðynne
THING   ðing (-) n.
THINK   hogian/ hycgan i, ii; ðencan i
THINK OUT   mamrian ii
THINNING   ðynnung (-a) f.
THIRD   ðridda
THIRST   ðurst m.
THIRST   ðyrstan i
THIRSTY   ðurstig
THIRTEEN   ðreotiene

THIRTEENTH   ðreoteoða
THISTLE   ðistel (ðistlas) m.
THITHER   ðider
THORN   bremel (-as) m.; ðorn (-as) m.
THORN BUSH   ðorn (-as) m.
THORNY   ðyren
THOUGH   ðeah av. conj.
THOUGHT   hyge m.; hygd (-u) f. n.; ðanc (-as, -u) m. n.; ðoht (-as) m.; ðeaht (-u) f. n.
THOUGHTFUL   ðancol
THOUSAND   ðusend (-u) n.
THREAT   beot (-) n.
THREATEN   hwopan 7; ðreagan ii; ðreatian ii
THREE   ðrie
THREE HUNDRED   ðreohund n. pl.
THREE-FOLD   ðrifeald
THRESH   ðerscan i
THRESHOLD   ðerscwold m.
THROAT   hrace (hracan) f.; woddor (-) n.
THRONE   stol (-as) m.
THRONG   geðrang (-) n.; ðraec (ðracu) n.
THROUGH   ðurh
THROW   weorpan 3; worpian ii
THROW AWAY   weorpan 3
THROWING   weorp n.
THRUST THROUGH   stingan 3
THULE   ðyle m.
THUNDER   ðunor m.
THUNDER   ðun(r)ian ii
THURSDAY   Thursdaeg (Thursdagas) m.; Þunresdaeg (Þunresdagas) m.
THUS   ðus
TICKLE   tinclian ii
TIDE   flod (-as) m.
TIE   tiegan i
TIE UP   bindan 3; wriðan 1
TIE WITH ROPE   raepan i; saelan i
TILE   tigel(e) (tigelan) f.
TILL   erian i
TIME   hwil (-a) f.; mael (-) n.; sael (-e) f.; sið (-as) m.; stund (-a) f.; tid (-a) f.; ðrag (-a) f.
TIME, HARD   ðrag (-a) f.
TIME OF DAY   daegmael (-) n.
TIMES, AT   hwilum av.; ðragum av.

TIMID   bleađ
TIRE   tierian ii; werigian ii
TIRE OF   đreotan 2
TIRED   međe; werig
TISSUE   webb (-) n.
TO   to
TO (TOWARD)   toweard
TOAD   tosca (-n) m.
TODAY   heodaeg; todaeg(e) a. av.
TOGETHER   aetgaedre; aetsamod; geador; samod;
    togaedre; tosamne
TOGETHER, BRING   samnian ii
TOGETHER, LIVING   samwist m. f.
TOIL   susl (-) n.; swinc (-) n.; đroht m.
TOIL   swencan i; swincan 3
TOILSOME   đroht; weorcsum
TOKEN   biecđ (-a) f.; tacen (-) n.
TONGUE   tunge (tungan) f.
TOO   to
TOOTH   tođ (teđ)
TOP   ypplen (-u) n.
TORMENT   orlege (orlegu) n.; susl (-) n.
TORMENT   waelan i
TORSO   hama (-n) m.; leap (-as) m.
TORTURE   tintreg (-u) n.
TOSSING OF WAVES   geweale (-) n.
TOUCH   felan i; hrinan 1
TOUCHING   getenge
TOWARD   togenes
TOWER   stiepel (stieplas) m.; torr (-as) m.
TOWER   hlifian ii
TOWERING   brant; steap
TOWN, LARGE   ceaster (ceastra) f.
TRACK   last (-as) m.; spor n.; swađu f.; trod
    (-u) n.
TRADE   ciepan i
TRAIL   last (-as) m.
TRANSITORY   hwilen; hwilwende; laen- pref.; laene
TRANSPORT   ferian i
TRANSVERSE đweorh
TRAPPINGS   fraetwa f. pl.; geatwe f. pl.
TRAVERSE   ofergan anv.; paeđđan i
TREAD   tredan 5; treddan i; treddian ii
TREASURE   gestreor (-) n.; hord (-as, -) m. n.;
    mađum (mađmas) m.; scaett (-as) m.;

TREASURE (CONTD.)   sinc (-) n.
TREASURES   fraetwa f. pl.
TREASURY   hord (-as, -) m. n.
TREAT (MEDICALLY)   lacnian ii
TREE   beam (-as) m.; treo (-wu, -) n.
TREMBLE   bifian ii; cwacian ii
TRIAL   fandung (-a) f.
TRIBE   maegð (-a) f.
TRIBUTE   gafol n.; gambe (gamban) f.
TRICK   hinderhoc m.; wrenc (-as) m.
TRINITY   ðrines f.
TRIP UP   hieltan i
TRIPLE   ðrifeald
TROOP   corðor (-) n.; heap (-as) m.; hloð (-a)
    f.; hos f.; hwearf (-as) m.; scalu f.;
    sweot (-) n.; trum (-) n.; weorod (-) n.;
    ðreat (-as) m.
TROUBLE   gnorn (-as) m.; gnyrn (-a) f.
TROUBLE   gemarian ii; lemman i; waegan i
TROUBLE ABOUT   reccan i
TROUBLED   droflic
TROUT   scot (-as) m.
TRUE   soð; treowe; waer
TRUMPET (WOODEN)   bieme (bieman) f.
TRUNK   hama (-n) m.; leap (-as) m.
TRUST   waer f.
TRUST   treowan i
TRUST IN   treowian ii
TRUTH   riht n.; soð n.; treowð (-a) f.
TRY   cunnian ii; fandian ii; fundian ii; neðan i
TRY TO GET   romian ii
TUESDAY   Tiwesdaeg (Tiwesdagas) m.
TUMOR   wenn (-as, -a) m. f.
TUMULUS   hlaw/hlaew (-as) m.
TUMULT   draeg n.; lac (-) n.; prass m.; storm
    (-as) m.
TUNIC   tunece (tunecan) f.
TURBULENCE   gebland n.
TURF   sweard (-as) m.; turf (tyrf) f.
TURN   cierr (-as) m.
TURN   bugan 2; cierran i; hweorfan 3; tyrnan i;
    wendan i; windan 3
TURN BACK   biegan i
TURN, IN   eft
TURNABOUT   wierp m.

81

TURTLE-DOVE   turtle (turtlan) f.
TUSK   tusc (-as) m.
TWELFTH   twelfta
TWELVE   twelf
TWENTY   twe(ge)ntig
TWIG   tan (-as) m.; telga (-n) m.; twig (-u) n.
TWILIGHT   glom m.; tweoneleoht (-) n.
TWINKLING OF AN EYE   eaganbearhtm (-as) m.
TWINS   getwinn (-as) m.
TWIST   windan 3; wraestan i; wrencan i; wriðan 1
TWO   twegen

U

UGLY   grislic
ULCER   blegen f.
UNASHAMED   unscamig
UNCANNY   unhiere
UNCERTAIN   tealt; tweonol; waefre
UNCLE, MATERNAL   eam (-as) m.
UNCLE, PATERNAL   faedera (-n) m.
UNCLEAN   unsyfre
UNCLEVER   aegiepe
UNDER   under
UNDERSTAND   ongietan 5
UNDERSTANDING   andgiet n.
UNDERTAKE   -ginnan 3
UNDERTAKING   anginn n.
UNFRIGHTENED   ungeblyged
UNIFORMLY   anfealdlice; endemes(t)
UNITE   geanlaecan i
UNLEARNED   laewede
UNLESS   nefne
UNMARRIED   hagusteald
UNREASONABLE   ungescad
UNREGRETFULLY   unmurnlice
UNTIL   oð; oððe; oððaet
UNTROUBLED   unmurnlic
UNUSUAL   anlic; seldlic
UNUSUALLY   seldlice
UP   upp av.; uppe av.
UP, DIRECTED   ufeweard a.
UPLAND   mor (-as) m.
UPON   uppan
UPPER   ufeweard; upplic

UPWARDS   uppweards
URGE   manian ii
URINATE   micgian ? ii?
URINATING   micgung (-a) f.
URINE   micga (-n) m.; micge (-an) f.
USE   bryce m.; nytt (-a) f.
USE   brucan 2; neotan 2; nyttian ii
USEFUL   behefe; bryce; gifre; nytt
USELESS   orfierme; unnyt(lic)
USELESS, BECOME   idlian ii
USUAL   genge; điewe
UTTERANCE   giedd (-) n.; spraec (-a) f.; word
   (-) n.

V

VACANT   idel
VAIN, IN   holunga
VALLEY   dael (dalu) n.; hop (-u) n.
VALOR   ellen n.
VALUE   weord n.
VANISH   swamian ii
VANQUISH   hnaegan i
VARIEGATED   mael
VARIOUS   mis(sin)lic
VARIOUSLY   mis(sin)lice
VARY   fagian ii
VAT   faet (fatu) n.
VAULT OVER   hwealfan i
VAULTING   hwealf (-a) f.
VEGETABLE   wyrt (-a) f.
VEHICLE   faer (faru) n.; scrid (-u) n.
VEIL   wrigels (-) n.
VEIN   aeder (aedra) f.; aedre (aedran) f.
VERDICT, JUDICIAL   dom (-as) m.; spraec (-a) f.
VERSE   fers (-) n.
VERSIFY   fersian ii
VERY   fela- pref.; regn- pref.; sare; swiđe;
   đearle
VESSEL   faer (faru) n.; faet (fatu) n.; fleot
   (-as) m.
VESSEL, SAILING   naca (-n) m.
VEXATION   anda m.; teon (-) n.; teona (-) m.
VIBRATION   geswing (-) n.
VICE   leahtor m.

VICINITY   neahwist m. f.
VICTORY   sige m.; sigor (-as) m.
VIGIL   waecce (waecca) f.
VIKING   wicing (-as) m.
VILLIFY   lean 6
VINEGAR   eced n.
VIOLENCE   haest (-a) f.
VIOLENT   deor; stearc; strang
VIRGIN   faemne (faemnan) f.
VIRTUOUS   cusc
VISE   clamm (-as) m.
VISIBLE   gesene; sewenlic
VISION   swefn (-) n.
VISIT   neosan i; neosian ii
VISITATION   socn (-a) f.
VISITOR   cuma (-n) m.; gaest- pref.; giest (-as)
    m.
VISOR   grima (-n) m.
VOICE   hleodor (-) n.; reord (-a) f.; stefn (-a)
    f.
VOMIT   spiwan 1
VOW   beot (-) n.
VOW   beotian ii

W

WADE   wadan 6
WADING PLACE   waed (wadu) n.
WAGON   waegn (-as) m.
WAIT   bidan 1
WAIT FOR   bidan 1
WAKEN   weccan i; wreccan i
WALK   gangan 7
WALKER   -genga (-n) m.
WALKING   fede n.
WALL   mur (-as) m.; wag/waeg (-as) m.; weall
    (-as) m.
WALLOW   wealwian ii
WANDER   aswaeman i; swician ii; wandrian ii
WANDERER   eardstapa (-n) m.; waeda (-n) m.
WANDERING OFF COURSE   aeflast m.
WANTON   gal
WANTONNESS   gal n.; gaelsa (-n) m.; wraenes f.
WANE   wanian ii
WANING   wanung (-a) f.

WARDEN   weard (-as) m.
WARFARE   guð f.; hild (-a) f.; wig (-) n.
WARLIKE   heaðu- pref.
WARM   wearm
WARM, BECOME   wearmian ii
WARM, MAKE   wierman i
WARN   wearnian ii
WARNING   wearnung (-a) f.
WARP   wefl (-a) f.
WARRIOR   beorn (-as) m.; cempa (-n) m.; dreng
     (-as) m.; eorl (-as) m.; freca (-n) m.;
     haeleð (-as) m.; hagusteald (-as) m.; oretta
     (-n) m.; scaða (-n) m.; secg (-as) m.; wiga
     (-n) m.; wigend (-) m.; wrecca (-n) m.
WARRIOR-BAND   dryht (-a) f.; ðreat (-as) m.
WARY   waer
WARY, BE   warian ii
WASH   ðwean 6; wascan 7
WASH DOWN   swillan i; swillian ii
WASHING   ðweal (-) n.
WASTE   ieðe; weste
WASTE AWAY   dwinan 1
WASTE, LAY   westan i
WASTELAND   westen (-as, -u) m. n.
WATCH   waecce (waecca) f.
WATCH   wacian ii
WATCH, KEEP   wacian ii
WATCH OVER   weardian ii
WATER   ear (-as) m.; flot n.; waed (wadu) n.;
     waeta m.; waeter (-) n.
WATER   leccan i
WAVE   haerm (-a) f.; hop (-as) m.; waðuma (-n)
     m.; waeg (-as) m.; yð (-a) f.
WAVERING   wancol; waefre
WAX   weax n.
WAY   -gang (-as) m.; lad (-a, -) f. n.; weg (-as)
     m.; wise (wisan) f.
WAY OF LIFE   folgað (-as) m.
WEAK   tydre; wac
WEAK, BECOME   weornian ii
WEAKEN   besylcan i; sleccan i; waecan i; wacian
     ii; wican 1
WEAKLY   wace
WEAKNESS   tydernes (-a) f.
WEALTH   feoh (-) n.; wela (-n) m.

85

WEALTHY, BE   spedan i
WEAPON   waepen (-) n.
WEAR   beran 4
WEARY   meðe; werig
WEATHER   weder (-) n.
WEAVE   webbian ii
WEB (OF FATE)   gewif (-u) n.
WED   weddian ii
WEDNESDAY   Wodnesdaeg (Wodnesdagas) m.
WEED   weod (-) n.
WEEK   wice/wicu (wican) f.
WEEP   greotan 2; reotan 2; wepan 7
WEEPING   wop (-as) m.
WEIGH DOWN   hlaestan i
WELL   faele; tela/tila; wel
WELL UP   weallan 7; wiellan i
WELL UP, CAUSE TO   seoðan 2
WELL-BEING   haelu f.; wist (-e) m. f.
WELLING UP   wielm (-as) m.
WELL-KNOWN   cnaewe
WELSHMAN   wealh (wealas) m.
WEST   west
WEST, FROM THE   westan
WESTMOST   westmest
WET   stieman i; waetan i; wesan i
WET   deawig; waet
WETNESS   waeta m.
WETTING   sype m.
WHALE   hranfix (-as) m.; hwael (hwalas) m.
WHAT   hwaet; ðe part.
WHAT KIND OF   hulic
WHEAT   corn n.; hwaet (-e) m.
WHEATEN   hwaeten
WHEEL   hweol (-) n.
WHEN   hwanne; ða; ðan; ðanne
WHENCE   hwanan
WHERE   hwaer; hwider; ðaer
WHERE, FROM   hwanan
WHEREFORE   forhwy
WHETHER   hwaeðere av. conj.
WHICH   ðe part.
WHICH OF TWO   hwaeðer a.
WHICHEVER OF TWO   swaeðer
WHILE   ðenden av. conj.
WHIP   swingel(le) (swingella) f.; swipa/swipu

WHIP (CONTD.)   (swipan, swipa) m. f.
WHIP   swipian ii
WHIRL UP   stincan 3
WHISPER   runian ii
WHISTLE   hwinan 1; hwistlian ii
WHITE (SHADE)   beorht; blac; hwit; leoht; scir
WHITE, GLOSSY   blanca
WHITEN   hwitan i
WHITHER   hwider
WHITTLE   ceorfan 3; ðwitan 1
WHO   hwa; ðe part.
WHOEVER   gehwa
WHOLE   gesund; hal; onwealg
WHY   hwy
WICKED   fracuð; fraetig; maene
WIDE   sid; wid
WIDELY   side; wide
WIDOW   wuduwe (wudewan) f.
WIELD POWER   wealdan 7; wieldan i
WIFE   bryd (-e) f.; wif (-) n.
WILD   grimm; reoc; wilde
WILL   willa (-n) m.
WILL   willan anv.; nyllan anv. neg.
WILLING   faegen
WIN   feohtan 3; gewinnan 3
WIND   wind (-as) m.
WINDOW   eagðyrel (-u) n.
WINDY   windig
WINE   win n.
WINE, NEW   must m.
WING   feðere (feðeru) n.
WINGS, PROVIDE WITH   feðerian ii
WINTER   missere (misseru) n.; winter (wintru) n.
WIRE, DRAWN   wir (-as) m.
WISDOM   snytru (snytre) f.; wisdom m.
WISE   frod; snotor; snytre; wis; wittig
WISE, BE   frodian ii; snytrian ii
WISH   will n.; willa (-n) m.; wilnung (-a) f.
WISH   willan anv.; nyllan anv. neg.; wilnian ii;
    wyscan i
WITH   mid
WITHDRAW   swaðrian /sweðrian ii
WITHER   forwisnian ii
WITHIN   innan
WITHIN, COMING FROM   innancund

87

WITHIN, DIRECTED TO   innanweard; inneweard
WITHOUT   -least/-liest suff.; wan- pref.
WITHOUT, FROM   utan
WIZARD   dry (-as) m.
WOBBLE   tealtrian ii
WOE   wa (-n) m.; wea (-n) m.
WOLF   wearg (-as) m.; wulf (-as) m.; wylf (-a) f.
WOLFISH   wylfen
WOMAN   bryd (-e) f.; wif (-) n.
WOMAN, SINGLE   maegeð (-a) f.
WOMAN, YOUNG   maegden (-u) n.
WOMB   innoð m. f.; hrif (-u) n.; wamb (-a) f.
WONDER   waefðu (waefða) f.; wundor (-) n.
WONDER   wundrian ii
WOOD   beam (-as) m.; holt (-) n.; treo (-) n.;
    wudu (wuda) m.
WOODED   wudig
WOODS   wudu (wuda) m.
WOODY   wudig
WOOF   wefl (-a) f.
WOOL   wull f.
WORD   word (-) n.
WORK   weorc (-) n.; wyrht (-a, -) f. n.
WORKER   wyrhta (-n) m.
WORLD   eorðe (eorðan) f.; middangeard (-as) m.;
    weorold (-a) f.
WORM   wyrm (-as) m.
WORMWOOD   wermod m.
WORRY   tiergan i
WOUND   benn (-a) f.; dolg (-) n.; laela (-n) m.;
    sar (-) n.; wund (-a) f.
WOUND   bennian ii; dolgian ii; sargian ii; sli-
    ðan i; taesan i; wundian ii
WOUNDED   wund
WOVEN WORK   webb (-) n.
WRAP   waefan i
WRAP UP   forðylmian i
WREATH   wraed/wraeð (-a) f.; wriða (-n) m.
WRENCH   scaenan i; wrencan i
WRETCH   ierming (-as) m.
WRETCHED   dreorig; earm; unlaed
WRETCHED, BE   dreorigian ii
WRETCHEDNESS   iermðu (iermða) f.
WRITE   writan 1
WRITE DOWN BRIEFLY   brefan i

WRITER   writere (writeras) m.
WRONG   unriht (-) n.
WRONG   dwol

Y Z

YAWN   ganian ii; -ginan 1
YEARN   giernan i; langian ii
YEAR   gear (-) n.; wintru m. pl.
YEARS OF ONE'S LIFE   ielde f. pl.
YEAST   beorma (-n) m.
YELLOW   geolu
YELLOW, GLOSSY   fealu
YELLOW-ORANGE   read
YESTERDAY   geostrandaeg; geostranniht
YET   gen; giet; ꝺagen; ꝺagiet
YEW TREE   iw (-) n.
YIELD   wican 1
YOKE   geoc (-u) n.
YOLK   geoloca (-n) m.
YORE, OF   geara; geo/iu
YOUNG   geong
YOUNG MAN   cild (-ru) n.; cniht (-as) m.; dreng
    (-as) m.; hyse (hyssas) m.
YOUNG WOMAN   meowle (meowlan) f.
YOUTH   geoguꝺ (-a) f.
ZEAL   eornost (-a) f.
ZEPHYR   zefferus m.

OLD ENGLISH-ENGLISH DICTIONARY

A

```
A     ever
ABBUD (-as) m.    abbot
ABYCGAN i    redeem
AC (aec) m.    oak tree
AC    but
ACAN 6    ache, hurt
ACLIAN ii    frighten
ACOL    frightened
ACWENCAN i    extinguish
AD (-as) m.    pyre
ADELA (-n) m.    dirt, dirty place
ADESA (-n) m.    adz, hatchet
ADIHTIAN ii    arrange
ADILEGIAN ii    blot out, erase
ADL (-a) f.    illness, infirmity
AFOL    n.    might, power
AFOR    bitter, fierce
AG- pref.    fearful, fearsome
AGAN prp.    have, possess, rule
AGEN a.    one's own
AGEND (-) m.    owner, ruler
AGLAECA (-n) m.    monster
AGNIAN ii    appropriate to oneself
AHNEOPAN 2    pick, pluck
AHYRIAN ii    hire
ALAN 6    grow
ALIEPE    alone
ALIESEND (-) m.    redeemer
ALIÞIAN ii    detach
AMASIAN ii    amaze
AMBIHT (-as) m.    messenger
AMBIHT (-u) n.    duty, function, office
AMEN    amen
AN a. pro.    one
ANA    alone
ANCOR (-as) m.    anchor
AND    and
ANDA m.    anger, vexation
ANDCWISS (-a) f.    reply
ANDETTAN i    acknowledge, confess, promise
ANDGIET n.    intelligence, understanding
ANDLEOFA (-n) m.    sustenance
```

ANDSACA (-n) m.   adversary
ANDSWARIAN ii   answer
ANDSWARU f.   answer
ANDWEARD   present
ANDWIST (-a) f.   support
ANDWLITA (-n) m.   countenance
ANFEALD   simple
ANFEALDLICE   uniformly
ANGA   only, sole
ANGINN n.   attack, beginning, undertaking
ANLIC   handsome, sole, solitary, unusual
ANLIEPE   solitary
ANPAEÐ (anpaðas) m.   narrow path
ANSTAPA (-n) m.   solitary one
ANUNGA/AENINGA   altogether, completely
AR (-as) m.   messenger
AR (-a) f.   benefit, favor, grace, honor
AR (-a) f.   oar
AR n.   copper
ARAEDNES (-a) f.   condition, stipulation
ARIAN ii   honor, respect
AROD   bold, swift
ASCIAN ii   ask
ASCUNG (-a) f.   inquiry
ASSA (-n) m.   ass, jackass
ASTIEPAN i   bereave
ASTIGAN 1   climb
ASWAEMAN i   mope, pine away, wander
ATOL   (-) n.   evil
ATOL   horrible
ATOR (-) n.   poison
AÐ (-as) m.   oath, pledge
AÐSWYRD (-) n.   oath
AWYRTWALIAN ii   root out

AE

AE f.   eternal law, right
AEBYLGÐ f.   anger
AECER (-as) m.   arable land, cultivated field
AECS (-a) f.   axe
AEDER (aedra) f.   artery, vein
AEDRE (aedran) f.   artery, vein
AEDRE   quickly
AEFAESTNES (-a) f.   religion

AEFEN (-) n.   eve, evening
AEFEST (-e) f.   disfavor, dislike
AEFESTIG   envious
AEFLAST m.   wandering off course
AEFTER   according to, after
AEFTERRA   next, second
AEFÞANCA m.   displeasure, offense
AEG (-ru) n.   egg
AEGHWA   anyone
AEGHWANAN   from anywhere
AEGHWAER   anywhere, everywhere
AEGHWAES   completely
AEGHWAEÐER   both, either, everyone
AEGHWIDER   in all directions
AEGHWILC   each
AEGIEPE   awkward, unclever
AEHT (-e) f.   possessions, property
AEL (-as) m.   eel
AELAN i   burn up, kindle
AELC   each
AELED m.   fire
AELF (ielfe, ylfe) m. f.   elf
AELMESSE (aelmessan) f.   alms, almsgiving
AELUNG (-a) f.   burning
AEMELNES (-a) f.   tastelessness
AEMETTE (aemettan) f.   ant
AEMETTIG   empty
AENIG   any
AENLIC   rare
AEPPEL (aepplas) m.   apple
AEPPLED   apple-shaped, embossed
AER   before, sooner
AERENDE (aerendu) n.   errand, message
AERENDIAN ii   take a message
AEREST   at first
AERING f.   daybreak
AERIST m. f. n.   resurrection
AERN (-) n.   building
AERN   early
AERNMORGEN (aernmorgnas) m.   early morning
AEROR av.   before
AES n.   carrion
AESC (-as) m.   ashwood, ashwood spear
AESCE (aescan) f.   inquiry
AESWIC (-as) m.   infamy, offense

AET m. f.   eating, food
AET   at, from
-AETA suff.   consuming, eater
AETGAEDRE   together
AETGRAEPE a.   seizing
AETLENGE   pertaining to
AETREN   poisonous
AETSOMOD   together
AEÞELE   noble
AEÞELIAN ii   ennoble
AEÞELING (-as) m.   nobleman, prince
AEÞELU f. n. pl.   lineage, nobility, the elite
AEÞM (-as) m.   breath
AEWAN i   despise, scorn
AEWISC f. n.   disgrace, shame

B

BAD f.   compulsion, force, levy
BAN (-) n.   bone
BANA (-n) m.   death, slayer
BAND (-as, -a) m. f.   fetter
BANN (-) n.   command, proclamation
BANNAN 7   proclaim
BASILISCA (-n) m.   basilisk
BASU   red-purple
BAT (-as) m.   boat
BATIAN ii   grow better
BAÞIAN ii   bathe
BAEC (bacu) n.   back
BAECLING   backwards
BAEDAN i   compel
BAEL n.   fire, flame, funeral pyre
BAELC (-as) m.   canopy, covering
BAER (-a) f.   bier
BAER   bare, exposed, naked
BAERNAN i   burn
BAETAN i   bite
BAETAN i   bridle, harness
BAEÞ (baþu) n.   bath
BE/BI   according to, beside
BEACEN (-) n.   sign
BEACNIAN ii   betoken, make a sign
BEACNUNG (-a) f.   indication
BEADU f.   battle

96

```
BEAG (-as) m.    ring
BEAGAS m. pl.    jewelry
BEALCETTAN i    belch
BEALCNIAN ii    belch
BEALD    bold, brave
BEALDIAN ii    be bold
BEALDOR (-as) m.    bold man, chieftan
BEALU (-) n.    evil, harm
BEAM (-as) m.    cross, tree, wood
BEARD (-as) m.    beard
-BEARD suff.    bearded
BEARM (-as) m.    bosom, chest, lap, middle
BEARM (-as) m.    possession
BEARN (-) m.    child
BEARU (bearwas) m.    grove
BEATAN 7    beat, strike
BEBOD (-) n.    command, commandment, order
BEBYCGAN i    sell
BED (-u) n.    prayer
BEDAELAN i    deprive of
BEDD (-) n.    bed
BEGEN    both
BEGIETAN 5    acquire, get
BEHEAFDIAN ii    behead
BEHEFE    fitting, useful
BEHOFIAN ii    require
BEHREOSIAN ii    repent
BELCEDSWEORA    swollen-necked
BELGAN 3    be angry, grow angry
BELIFD    dead
BEN (-e) f.    petition
BENA (-n) m.    petitioner, suppliant
BENC (-a) f.    bench
BEND (-as, -a) m. f.    bond
BENN (-a) f.    wound
BENNIAN ii    wound
BENSIAN ii    entreat
BEO (-n) f.    bee
BEODAN 2    command, offer
BEON anv.    be
BEOR n.    beer
BEORCAN 3    bark
BEORG (-as) m.    defense, hill, mountain
BEORGAN 3    conceal, protect
BEORHT    bright, fair, white
```

BEORHTIAN ii   sound clearly, sound out
BEORMA (-n) m.   yeast
BEORN (-as) m.   warrior, young man
BEORSCIP (-an) m.   merriment
BEOT (-) n.   promise, threat, vow
BEOTIAN ii   vow
BERA (-n) m.   bear
BERAN 4   bear, bring, carry, wear
BERE (beran) f.   covering
BERIAN i   make bare, expose
BERIEFAN i   plunder, rob
BERSTAN 3   burst
BESCITAN 1   shit
BESTREÞÞAN i   bedeck, bestrew
BESYLCAN i   exhaust, weaken
BET av.   better
BETAN i   atone for, improve
BETERA a.   better
BETLIC   splendid
BETST   best
BETWEON   between
BETWEONUM   between
BETWEOX   between
BEÞIAN ii   foment
BEWADEN   issued from
BID n.   delay, halt
BIDAN 1   wait, wait for
BIDDAN i-5   ask, order, pray
BIDUNG (-a) f.   abode
BIECÞ (-a) f.   sign, token
BIEGAN i   bend, blunt, turn back
BIELC m.   pride
BIELCAN i   belch
BIELDAN i   embolden, encourage
BIELDU (-) f.   boldness
BIEME (bieman) f.   wooden trumpet
BIERGAN i   eat, taste
BIERHTAN i   brighten
BIERHTU (-) f.   brightness
BIERMAN i   swell
BIERNAN 3   burn
BIERWAN i   prepare, polish
BIEWEND (-) m.   polisher
BIFIAN ii   tremble
BILEWIT   innocent, pure

BILL (-) n.   sword
BIND (-) n.   bond, constraint, fetter
BINDAN 3   bind, freeze, tie up
BINDERE (binderas) m.   binder, one who binds
BINN (-a) f.   manger
BIRIHTE   next to
BISCOP (-as) m.   bishop
BISIG   busy
BISIGIAN ii   occupy oneself, be busy or bad in a
      desperate way
BISIGU (bisiga) f.   business, preoccupation
BISMER m. f. n.   derision, insult, mockery, scorn
BISMERIAN ii   despise, mock, scorn
BISPELL (-) n.   parable
BITAN 1   bite, cut
BITE (-) m.   cut
BITER   cutting, sharp
BITERE   cruelly, sharply
BLAC   bright, light, white
BLACERN n.   lantern
BLACIAN ii   turn pale
BLANCA (-n) m.   white horse
BLANCA   glossy white
BLAND n.   turbulence
BLANDAN 7   mingle, mix
BLAT(E)   livid, pale
BLATIAN ii   turn pale
BLAWAN 7   blow
BLAEC   black, dull black, dark
BLAECAN i   bleach
BLAED (-as) m.   glory, prosperity; spirit
BLAED (-a) f.   foliage
BLAED (bladu) n.   leaf
BLAEST (-as) m.   blast, blowing
BLAETAN i   bleat
BLEAÐ   gentle, shy, timid
BLED (-a) f.   foliage, fruit
BLEDAN i   bleed
BLEGEN f.   blister, ulcer
BLENCAN i   cheat, deceive
BLENDAN i   deceive, make blind
BLEO (-) m.   color
BLETSIAN ii   bless, consecrate
BLETSUNG (-a) f.   blessing
BLICAN 1   shine

99

BLIND   blind
BLINNAN 3   cease, stop
BLISS (-a) f.   gaiety, happiness
BLISSUNG (-a) f.   rejoicing
BLIĐE   happy, happily
BLOD (-) n.   blood
BLODIG   bloody
BLODIGIAN ii   make bloody
BLOSTM (-as, -a) m. f.   bloom
BLOSTMA (-n) m.   bloom
BLOT (-) n.   sacrifice
BLOTAN 7   sacrifice
BLOWAN 7   bloom, flourish
BOC (bec) f.   book
BOCBLAEC n.   ink
BOCERE (boceras) m.   scholar
BOCFELL (-) n.   paper, parchment
BOCGESAMNUNG (-a) f.   library
BODA (-n) m.   messenger
BODIAN ii   announce, preach, relate
BODUNG (-a) f.   message
BOG (-as) m.   arm, shoulder
BOGA (-n) m.   bow, weapon
BOLCA (-n) m.   gang-plank
BOLD (-) n.   building
BOLLA (-n) m.   cowl; cup
BOLSTER (bolstras) m.   cushion
BORA (-n) n.   bearer, carrier
BORD (-) n.   board, plank; shield; side of a
    ship
BOREN   begotten, born
BOSM (-as) m.   bosom
BOT (-a) f.   atonement, remedy
BOTM m.   bottom
BRAD   broad
BRAND (-as) m.   burning wood, flame
BRAND (-as) m.   sword
BRANT   towering
BRASTELIAN ii   roar
BRASTL m.   crackling
BRASTLIAN ii   crackle
BRAEDAN i   spread abroad, spread out
BRAEDING (-a) f.   roast meat
BRAEDU f.   breadth
BRAEGD (-as) m.   brandishing, quick movement

100

BRAEMEL (-as) m.　bramble
BRAESNE　strong
BRAEW (-as) m.　brow
BREAHT (-as) m.　noise
BREAHTM (-as) m.　brightness, flashing
BREC (-) n.　breaking
BRECAN 5/4　break
BRECØ (-a) f.　heartbreak
BRECØA (-n) m.　broken condition; sorrow
BREDIAN ii　regenerate, restore
BREDWIAN ii　strike down
BREFAN i　write down briefly
BREGAN i　terrify
BREGDAN 3　draw a sword, move quickly
BREGO m.　lord, protector, ruler
BREME　famous, illustrious
BREMEL (-as) m.　thorn
BRENTING (-as) m.　high-prowed ship
BREORD (-as) m.　edge
BREOST (-) n.　breast, chest, heart
BREOTAN 2　break
BREOØAN 2　come to grief, perish
BRERD (-as) m.　point
BRESNE　strong
BREØ (-a) f.　grief
BRIDD (-as) m.　bird
BRIGD (-) n.　change of color
BRIGD m.　play of color
BRIGDELS (-as) m.　bridle
BRIM (-u) n.　edge, sea, seacoast, shore
BRINGAN i　bring
BROC (-as) m.　brook, stream
BROGA (-n) m.　terror
BROSNIAN ii　decay, disintegrate, perish
BROSNUNG (-a) f.　corruption, decay
BROØOR (broðru, -) m.　brother
BRU (-a) f.　eyelash
BRUCAN 2　enjoy, use
BRUN　bright, glossy brown, glistening
BRUNBASU　glossy reddish-brown
BRUNWAN(N)　dull brown
BRYCE m.　service, use
BRYCE　fragile; useful
BRYCG (-a) f.　bridge
BRYCGAN i　make a bridge

BRYCGIAN ii   bridge
BRYD (-e) f.   bride, wife, woman
BRYDGUMA (-n) m.   bridegroom
BRYDØING (-) n.   marriage ceremony
BRYNE m.   burning
BRYRDAN i   incite, prod
BRYSAN i   crush, pound
BRYTNIAN ii   divide, divide up
BRYTTA (-n) m.   dispenser, distributor
BRYTTIAN ii   break up, distribute
BU- pref.   settlement
BUAN 7/iii   dwell, settle
BUGAN 2   bend, retreat, turn
BUR (-as) m.   apartment, sleeping quarters, room
BURG (burig) f.   stronghold
BURNA (-n) m.   brook
BURNE (burnan) f.   brook
BUTAN   except, outside of
BYCGAN i   buy
BYDEN (-a) f.   bushel, measure
BYDENFAET (bydenfatu) n.   bushel
BYLDA (-n) m.   builder
BYRD (-a) f.   birth, nature by birth
BYRDU f.   race, nature by birth
BYRE (byras) m.   event, happening
BYRE (byras, -) m.   son
BYRELE (byrelas) m.   cupbearer
BYRELIAN ii   pour a drink
BYRGAN i   bury
BYRGEN (byrgna) f.   grave
BYRGEND (-as) m.   burier, gravedigger
BYRIAN i   be suitable
BYRIAN i   happen
BYRNE (byrnan) f.   byrnie, corslet
BYRST (-as) m.   damage, harm
BYSEN (bysna) f.   example

C

CAF   active, bold
CALCRAND   horse-shoe edged, shod
CALEND (-as) m.   month
CALIC (-as) m.   chalice
CALU   bald
CAMP (-as) m.   battle, fight

CAMPIAN ii   fight for
CANDEL (-a) f.   candle, light
CANTIC (-as) m.   canticle, chant
CARCAERN n.   prison
CARIAN ii   be anxious, suffer distress
CARIG   anxious
CARR (-as) m.   rock
CARU (cara) f.   anxiety, care, distress
CASERE (caseras) m.   emperor
CATT (-as) m.   cat
CATTE (cattan) f.   cat
CAEG (-a) f.   key
CAEGE (caegan) f.   key
CAELAN i   cool off
CEAFL (-as) m.   jaw
CEAFOR (-as) m.   beetle, chaffer, insect
CEALD   cold
CEALF (-ru) m.   calf
CEALLIAN ii   call
CEAP (-as) m.   bargain, business transaction,
    price
CEAPIAN ii   buy, do business
CEAPSTOW (-a) f.   market
CEAPUNG (-a) f.   business transaction
CEASTER (ceastra) f.   city, large town
CEDER   m. f. n.   cedar
CEMPA (-n) m.   fighter, warrior
CENE   bold
CENNAN i   bear a child, beget
CENÞU (cenða) f.   boldness
CEOL (-as) m.   ship
CEOLE (ceolan) f.   gorge
CEORFAN 3   cut, whittle
CEORL (-as) m.   churl, freeman, husbandman
CEOSAN 2   choose, elect, select
CEOWAN 2   chew
CHERUBIN   cherubim
CIEGAN i   call, call out
CIELE m.   chill, coolness
CIEPAN i   do business, trade
CIERMAN i   cry out, make a noise
CIERR (-as) m.   turn
CIERRAN i   convert, turn
CILD (-ru) n.   young man
CILDHAD (-as) m.   childhood

CILDISC   as or like a child, childish
CINNAN 3   destroy
CINNBAN (-) n.   jawbone
CIRCUL (-as) m.   circle
CIRICE (cirican) f.   church
CIRM (-as) m.   cry, noise
CIÞ (-as) m.   seed
CLAMM (-as) m.   grip, hand, vise
CLAÞ (-as) m.   cloth, clothes
CLAWU (clawa) f.   claw
CLAENE   clean, pure
CLAENSIAN ii   cleanse, purify
CLEA (-n) f.   claw
CLEMMAN i   chain, chut up
CLEOFAN 2   cleave, split
CLEOPIAN ii call, cry out
CLIBBOR   clinging, sticky
CLIEWEN n.   ball, heap, mass
CLIF (-u) n.   cliff
CLIFAN 1   stick
CLINGAN 3   shrink down into
CLIPIAN ii   call out
CLUD (-as) m.   mass of rocks
CLUS (-a) f.   enclosure
CLUSTOR (clustru) n.   bolt, lock
CLYMMIAN ii   climb, mount
CLYMPRE (clympras) m.   lump of metal
CLYPPAN i   embrace
CLYSAN i   close, shut
CNAWAN 7   know, recognize
CNAEWE   evident, well-known
CNEAR (-as) m.   ship
CNEO (-) n.   knee
CNEORISN (-a) f.   generation
CNEORISS (-a) f.   generation
CNIHT (-as) m.   young man
CNOLL (-as) m.   hill, knoll
CNOSL n.   family, relatives
CNOSSIAN ii   knock, pound
CNYSSAN i   knock against, strike
COC (-as) m.   chef, cook
COCERPANNE f.   cooking pan
CODOR (-as) m.   enclosure
COFA (-n) m.   closet, enclosed place
COHHETTAN i   clear the throat, cough

COL (-u) n.   coal, ember
COL   cool
COLIAN ii   cool off, freeze
COMETA (-n) m.   comet
CORN n.   grain, wheat
CORÐOR (-) n.   troop
COSS (-as) m.   kiss
COSTIAN ii   tempt
COST(N)UNG (-a) f.   temptation
COÐLICE   miserably, sickly
CRAEFT (-) n.   power, strength
CRAEFTIG   potent, powerful
CRAET (cratu) n.   cart
CREOPAN 2   creep
CRIBB (-a) f.   manger
CRINGAN 3   fall in battle
CRISTALLA (-n) m.   crystal
CRISTEN   Christian
CROG (-as) m.   pitcher
CRUDAN 2   crowd, press
CU (cy, cye) f.   cow
CUBUTERE f.   butter
CULFER/CULFRE (culfran) f.   dove
CULPE (culpan) f.   fault
CUMA (-n) m.   comer, visitor
CUMAN 4   come, go
CUMBOL (-) n.   banner, battle standard, ensign
-CUND suff.   coming from
CUNIAN ii   find out
CUNNAN prp.   know
CUNNIAN ii   attempt, tempt, try
CUNNUNG (-a) f.   temptation
CUSC   chaste, virtuous
CUÐ   certain, familiar, known
CUÐE   clearly
CWACIAN ii   quake, tremble
CWALU f.   death, killing, murder
CWANIAN ii   lament
CWEALM (-as) m.   death, killing
CWEARTAERN n.   prison
CWECCAN i   shake
CWEDOL   eloquent, talkative
CWELAN 4   die, kill, put to death
CWELLERE (cwelleras) m.   executioner, murderer
CWEMAN i   please

105

CWEME   pleasing
CWEN (-e) f.   queen
CWEÞAN 5   say
CWIC   alive, living
CWICIAN ii   bring into life, quicken
CWIDE (-) n.   saying
CWIELD   m. f. n.   death, destruction
CWIELMAN i   kill
CWIÞAN i   bewail, lament
CYCENE (cycenan) f.   kitchen
CYLL (-a) f.   leather bottle
CYME (cymas) m.   arrival, coming; lineage
CYME (cyma) f.   origin
CYME   fair, lovely
CYND (-e, -) f. n.   family
CYNE- pref.   royal
CYNELIC   royal
CYNEROF   noble
CYNING (-as) n.   king
CYNN (-) n.   family, race
CYPERA (-n) m.   spawning salmon
CYPPAN i   bind
CYRE (-) m.   choice
CYRTEN   beautiful, fair
CYSPAN i   fetter
CYSSAN i   kiss
CYST (-e) f.   choicest, the elite
CYST   excellent
CYSTIG   choice, good
CYTA (-n) m.   kite (bird of prey)
CYÞAN i   make known
CYÞIG   aware, knowing
CYÞÞ(U) (cyðða) f.   home, native land

D

DAFEN   suitable
DAFENIAN ii   befit, be suitable
DAGIAN ii dawn
DAL (-) n.   distribution, division, partition,
    separation, sharing
DAROÞ (-as) m.   dart, spear
DARU (dara) f.   harm, misfortune, woe
DAED (-e) f.   action, deed
DAEG (dagas) m.   day

```
DAEGHWAEMLICE    daily
DAEGMAEL (-) n.    time of day
DAEGRAED (-) n.    dawn
DAEL (-as) m.    part, portion, share
DAEL (dalu) n.    dale, valley
DAELAN i    apportion, divide, mete out, share
DAERST(E) f.    ferment, leaven
DEAD    dead
DEAF    deaf
DEAGAN 7    hide
DEAGOL/DEOGOL    concealed, dark
DEALL    proud
DEAÞ (-as) m.    death
DEAW m.    dew
DEAWIG    dewy, wet
DELFAN 3    dig
DEMA (-n) m.    judge
DEMAN i    judge
DEMEND m.    God
DENN (-) n.    den, lair
DEOFOL (deoflas) m.    devil
DEOP (-) n.    abyss
DEOP    deep
DEOPE    deeply, profoundly
DEOR (-) n.    animal
DEOR    bold, violent
DEORC    dark
DERIAN ii    harm, injure
DIEFAN i    dip, immerse
DIEGAN i    carry out, escape, endure, survive
DIEGLAN i    hide
DIEGLE    secretly
DIERAN i    praise
DIERE    dear, precious
DIERLING (-as) m.    dear one, favorite
DIERNAN i    conceal, keep secret
DIERNE    concealed, hidden, secret
DIERSIAN ii    glorify
DIMM    dark, dim
DIMMIAN ii    dim
DISC (-as) m.    dish, plate
DOGOR (-) m. n.    day
DOL    foolish
DOLG (-) n.    wound
DOLGIAN ii    wound
```

107

DOM (-as) m.   decision about, doom, Judgment Day,
    judicial verdict, opinion
DOMIAN ii   glorify
DON anv.   do, insert
DOR (-u) n.   gate, portal
DRACA (-n) m.   dragon
DRAGAN 6   beguile
DRAEDAN 7   dread
DRAEFAN i   drive away, exile
DRAEG n.   crowd, tumult
DREAM (-as) m.   gaiety, happiness, merriment
DRECCAN i   annoy, oppress
DREFAN i   disturb, excite
DRENCAN i   drink, cause to drink, drown
DRENG (-as) m.   warrior, young man
DREOGAN 2   do, experience, suffer
DREOPIAN ii   drip
DREOR m.   blood, gore
DREORIG   bloody, dreary, gory, mournful, wretched
DREORIGIAN ii   be sad, be wretched
DREORUNG (-a) f.   dropping, falling
DREOSAN 2   crumble, disintegrate, fall
DREPAN 5   strike
DREPE (drepas) m.   blow
DRIEMAN i   rejoice
DRIFAN 1   drive, drive on, proceed
DRINC/DRYNC (-as) m.   drink
DRINCAN 3   drink
DROFLIC   troubled
DROHT m. n.   condition of life, station in life
DROHTAÞ m.   usual experience, way of life
DROHTIAN ii   conduct oneself
DROPA (-n) m.   drop
DROPETTAN i   drip, drop
DROPUNG (-a) f.   dripping
DRUGIAN ii   become dry
DRUNCENNES f.   drunkenness
DRUSIAN ii   droop
DRY (-as) m.   magician, wizard
DRYCRAEFT (-as) m.   magic
DRYGAN i   dry, dry up
DRYGE   arid, dry
DRYHT (-a) f.   band of retainers, force, multi-
    tude, warrior-band
DRYHTEN (dryhtnas) m.   powerful lord

DRYRE m.   fall
DRYSMIAN ii   grow dark
DUFAN 2   dive
DUGAN prp.   be good, be good for something
DUGUÞ (-a) f.   excellence
DUMB   dumb, speechless
DUN (-a) f.   hill
DUNG (dyng) f.   prison
DUNN   dull brown
DURRAN prp.   dare
DURU (dura) f.   door, gate
DUST n.   dust
DWAES   foolish, stupid
DWAESCAN i   extinguish
DWELLAN i   hinder, mislead, prevent
DWEORG (-as) m.   dwarf
DWIELD (-) n.   error, heresy
DWINAN 1   disappear, waste away
DWOL a. pref.   silly, wrong
DWOLA (-n) m.   error, heresy
DWOLIAN ii   err
DWOLIC   crazy, mad, foolish
DWOLMA m.   chaos, confusion
DYHTIG   doughty, strong
DYNE m. n.   din
DYNIAN i   make a din
DYNT (-as) m.   blow, stroke
DYPPAN i   dip, immerse
DYRSTIG   daring
DYSIG   foolish
DYSIGIAN ii   act foolishly, err
DYTTAN i   close, stop up

E

EAC   also
EACA (-n) m.   increase
EACEN   large, pregnant
EACNIAN ii   become pregnant, grow large
EACNUNG (-a) f.   conception
EAD   blessed, lucky
EADEN   granted
EADIG   fortunate, happy
EAFORA (-n) m.   heir
EAFOÞ (-u) n.   power, strength

EAGANBEARHTM (-as) m.   twinkling of an eye
EAGE (eagan) n.   eye
EAGØYREL (-u) n.   window
EAHTA   eight, eighth
EAHTIAN ii   deliberate, esteem
EAHTLE (eahtlan) f.   esteem
EAHTTEOÞA   eighteenth
EAHTUNG (-a) f.   deliberation
EALA   alas!
EALD   old
EALDIAN ii   grow old
EALDOR (ealdras) m.   leader, lord of life
EALDOR (-) n.   condition or state of being alive,
    life
EALGIAN ii   defend
EALH (-as) m.   pagan temple
EALL   all, altogether, everything
EALLES   entirely
EALLUNGA   altogether, entirely
EALNEG   always
EALU m. n.   ale
EAM (-as) m.   maternal uncle
EAR (-as) m.   sea, water
EARC (-a) m. f.   storage chest
EARCE f.   ark, chest
EARD (-as) m.   home, land, place, yard
EARDIAN ii   dwell
EARDSTAPA (-n) m.   wanderer
EARE (earan) n.   ear
EARENDEL m.   rising sun
EARFOÞ (-u) n.   difficulty, hardship
EARFOÞLIC   difficult
EARM (-as) m.   arm (anatomical)
EARM   poor, wretched
EARNIAN ii   earn, merit
EARNUNG (-a) f.   desert; merit
EARP   dark
EAST   east
EASTAN   from the east
EASTERNE   eastern, oriental
EASTEWEARD   eastern, oriental
EAÞ   easily
EAÞE   easily
EAWUNGA   face to face
EAX f.   axle

110

EAXL (-a) f.   shoulder
EBBA m.   ebb-tide
EBBIAN ii   ebb, flow out
ECE   eternal
ECED n.   vinegar
ECG (-a) f.   edge
EDBYRDAN i   generate
EDISC (-as) m.   enclosed pasture
EDSCAEFT f.   regeneration
EDWIT (-) n.   blame, reproach
EFEN   equal, even with, level, parallel, smooth
EFENE   even, just
EFENETTAN i   make equal
EFNAN i   accomplish, achieve, make
EFSIAN ii   cut the hair of
EFSTAN i   hasten
EFT   again, in turn, later
EGE m.   fear, terror
EGESA (-n) m.   terror
EGESIAN ii   terrify
EGESIG   terrible, terrifying
EGLAN i   grieve, molest
EGLE   hateful
EHTAN i   follow after, persecute
EHTNES (-a) f.   persecution
EL(E)- pref.   from elsewhere
ELE m.   oil
ELLCOR   otherwise
ELLEN n.   strength, valor
ELLES   else, otherwise
ELLESHWERGEN   elsewhere
ELLNE   quickly
ELLNIAN ii   comfort; emulate
ELLOR   elsewhere
ELPEND (-) m.   elephant
ELÞEODIG   foreign
ENDE (endas) m.   end, seacoast
ENDEMES(T)   equally, uniformly
ENDIAN ii   end
ENDLEOFAN   eleven
ENDWERC (-) n.   pain in the ass
ENGE   anxious, confined, hard, narrow, painful,
    severe
ENGEL (englas) m.   angel
ENGU (enge) f.   confinement, narrowness

ENT (-as) m.   giant
ENTISC   gigantic
EODOR (-as) m.   protection, protector
EOFOR (-as) m.   boar
EOH m.   steed
EORL (-as) m.   earl, noble warrior
EORN (-as) m.   eagle
EORNOST (-a) f.   earnestness, zeal
EOROD n.   band of horsemen
EORÞE (eorðan) f.   earth
EOSOL (-as) m.   ass, donkey
EOTEN (-as) m.   giant
EOTENISC   gigantic
EOWDE f.   flock of sheep
EPISTOLA (-n) m.   letter, message
ERIAN i   till
ERINACES   hedgehogs
ESNE (esnas) m.   man, servant
EST (-e) f.   favor, grace
ESTE   gracious, kindly
ESTIG   gracious
ETAN 5   corrode, eat
EÞEL (eðlas) m.   inherited estate, native land

F

FACEN (-) n.   deceit
FAG   colored, stained
FAGIAN ii   change, vary
FAH   hostile
FAM n.   foam
FAMIG   foamy
FAMIGAN ii   foam
FANA (-n) m.   flag
FANDIAN ii   attempt, try
FANDUNG (-a) f.   trial
FARAN 6   die; go, journey
FAROÞ (-as) m.   beach
FAEC (facu) n.   interval of time
FAECNE   deceitful
FAEDER (-) m.   father
FAEDERA (-n) m.   paternal uncle
FAEDEREN- pref.   paternal
FAEGE   doomed, fated to die
FAEGEN   glad, willing

FAEGENIAN ii   rejoice
FAEGER   fair, lovely
FAEGERIAN ii   become beautiful
FAEHØ(U) (faehða) f.   crime, feud, hostility,
   revenge
FAELE   faithful, faithfully, good, well
FAELSIAN ii   cleanse, purify
FAEMAN i   foam
FAEMNE (faemman) f.   virgin
FAER m.   danger, sudden attack
FAER (faru) n.   expedition
FAER (faru) n.   vehicle, vessel
FAERAN i   frighten
FAERELD (-u) n.   journey
FAERINGA   suddenly
FAERSCEATT (-as) m.   fare
FAEST   firm, fixed
-FAEST suff.   firm in, fixed in
FAESTE   firmly, fixedly
FAESTEN (-) n.   fastness, prison, stronghold
FAESTNIAN ii   fasten, secure
FAESTNUNG (-a) f.   security
FAET (fatu) n.   container, cup, vat, vessel
FAET (-) n.   ornament, plate-metal
FAETED   ornamented
FAETELS m.   bag, receptacle
FAEÞM (-as) m.   bosom, embrace, protection
FAEÞMAN i   embrace, surround
FAEÞMIAN ii   embrace, surround
FEA (-n) m.   joy
FEA a.   few, a few
FEA av.   little
FEAHWON   a few
-FEALD suff.   -fold
FEALDAN 7   fold
FEALLAN 7   fall
FEALU   dark; glossy yellow
FEALWIAN ii   grow dark
FEARM (-as) m.   cargo, freight
FEARN (-) n.   fern
FEAX n.   hair
-FEAX suff.   -haired
FEDAN i   feed, nurture, raise
FEFER m. n.   fever
FEGAN i   fit together, join

113

FELA   many, much of
FELA- pref.   very
FELAN i   feel, touch
FELD (-as) m.   open country
FELL   cruel, fierce
FENG (-as) m.   grasp, grip
FENGEL (fenglas) m.   prince, tribal or political
    lord
FENN (-as) m.   fen, marsh
FEOH (-) n.   property, wealth
FEOHT (-) n.   battle, fight
FEOHTAN 3   fight, win
FEOHTE (feohta) f.   battle, fight
FEOL (-a) f.   file, rasp
FEOLAN 3   penetrate
FEON i   hate
FEON 5   rejoice
FEOND (-as, fiend) m.   enemy, fiend, Satan
FEORH (feoras, -) m. n.   life, life lived (and
    lost), spirit
FEORM (-a) f.   possession; sustenance
FEORMEND (-) m.   cleaner, polisher
FEORMIAN ii   clean, polish, scour
FEORMIAN ii   entertain, feed
FEORR   apart, far
FEORRAN   from afar
FEORRSIAN ii   depart, separate
FEO(WE)RÐA   fourth
FEOWER   four
FEOWERTIENE   fourteen
FEOWERTIG   forty
FEOWUNG (-a) f.   rejoicing
FERAN i   go, journey
FEREND (-) m.   messenger, sailor
FERHÐ (-as, -) m. n.   life, mind, spirit, spirit
    of
FERIAN i   transport
FERING (-a) f.   journey
FERS (-) n.   verse
FERSC   fresh
FERSIAN ii   versify
FETEL (-as) m.   belt
FETERA f. pl.   bonds, fetters
FETERIAN ii   fetter
FETIAN ii   fetch

FEÞA (-n) m.   foot-soldier, infantryman
FEÞE n.   gait, pace, one step, walking
FEÞER (-a) f.   feather
FEÞERE (feðeru) n.   wing
FEÞERIAN ii   feather, provide with wings
FEÞRIAN ii   provide with feathers, provide with
     wings
FIELL (-as) m.   death, fall
FIELLAN i   fell, kill
FIERD (-a) f.   armed force, defending army,
     militia
FIERRAN i   remove to afar
FIF   five
FIFEL (-) n.   sea-monster
FIFTA   fifth
FIFTIENE   fifteen
FIFTIG   fifty
FINDAN 3   find, invent
FINGER (fingras) m.   finger
FINOL m.   fennel
FINTA (-n) m.   consequence; tail
FIREN (-a) f.   crime
FIRENIAN ii   commit a crime
FIRST (-a) f.   ceiling
FISC (-as) m.   fish
FITT (-a) f.   poem, song
FITT (-) n.   contest,fight
FLA (-n) f.   arrow
FLACOR   flying
FLAGA (-n) m.   flier
FLAH   deceitful, hostile
FLAN (-a) f.   arrow
FLAESC n.   flesh
FLEAM (-as) m.   flight to safety
FLEAN 6   flay
FLEAX n.   flax
FLEDE   flooded, flooding, overflowing
FLEOGAN 2   fly
FLEOGE (fleogan) f.   fly, flying insect
FLEON 2   flee
FLEOT (-as) m.   raft, vessel
FLEOTAN 2   float, swim
FLETT (-) n.   floor of a hall or common room
FLIEMA (-n) m.   fugitive, refugee
FLIEMAN i   put to flight, rout

FLIES n.   fleece
FLINT (-as) m.   flint
FLITAN 1   compete, contend
FLOCAN 7   applaud, clap
FLOD (-as) m.   flood, sea, tide
FLOR (-as) m.   bottom, floor
FLOT n.   sea, water
FLOTA (-n) m.   floater, sailor, ship
FLOWAN 7   flow
FLYGE m.   flight of a bird
FLYHT (-as) m.   flight of a bird
FNAED (fnadu) n.   border, fringe
FNAEST m.   blast, breath
FODOR m.   food
FOG (-) n.   fitting, joint
FOLC (-) n.   people
FOLDE (foldan) f.   soil, earth
FOLGAÐ (-as) m.   comitatus, following, retinue,
    way of life
FOLGERE (folgeras) m.   followers, retainers
FOLGIAN ii   follow
FOLM (-a) f.   hand
FON 7   grasp, seize
FOR prep.   before, for
FOR conj.   because
FORAN av. prep.   before, forward, in front of
FORE   beforehand
FORERYNEL (-as) m.   forerunner; morning star
FOREWEARD   toward the future
FORGIEFAN 5   forgive, forget, give
FORGIEFNES (-a) f.   gift
FORHAEFEDNES f.   abstinence, self-restraint
FORHOGODNES f.   contempt
FORHT   afraid, frightened
FORHTFUL   fearful
FORHTIAN ii   become frightened
FORHTIG   afraid, frightened
FORHTUNG (-a) f.   fear
FORHWON conj.   because
FORHWY   wherefore
FORHYLMAN i   refuse obedience to
FORLAETAN 7   abandon, forsake
FORMA   first, foremost
FORPYNDAN i   do away with, remove
FORSETENES (-a) f.   purpose

116

FORST (-as) m.   frost
FORÞ   forward, keep on (with verb), onward
     (space and time)
FORÞBAERE   productive
FORÞYLMAN i   enclose, wrap, wrap up
FOR(E)WEARD a. av.   toward the future
FORWISNIAN ii   dry up, shrivel, wither
FORWOREN   decrepit
FOSTOR m.   food, sustenance
FOSTRIAN ii   nourish
FOT (fet) m.   foot
FOTLAST (-as) m.   footprint
FOTSCEAMOL (-as) m.   footstool
FOX (-as) m.   fox
FRACUÞ   hateful, wicked
FRAM   active, bold, brave
FRAM prep.   away from, concerning
FRANCA (-n) m.   Frankish spear
FRASIAN ii   ask, require
FRASUNG (-a) f.   question
FRAECNE   dangerous
FRAEGN m. n.   question
FRAETE   perverse, proud
FRAETIG   proud, wicked
FRAETWA f. pl.   trappings, treasures
FREA (-n) m.   creator, lord
FREC   greedy
FRECA (-n) m.   warrior
FRECGAN i-5   inquire
FREFRAN i   console, help
FREME   excellent, good, kind
FREMMAN i   accomplish, do
FREMSUM   gracious, kind
FREM(E)ÞE   alien, foreign
FREMU (frema) f.   excellence, goodness, kindness
FREO   free, generous, noble
FREOD (-a) f.   love, peace
FREODOM (-as) m.   freedom, free will
FREO(GA)N i   love
FREOND (-as, friend) m.   friend
FREORIG   freezing cold
FREOSAN 2   freeze
FRETAN 5   break; devour, eat
FRICCA (-n) m.   herald
FRICGAN i-5   ask

FRICLAN i   desire
FRIGAN 3   inquire
FRIGEDAEG (Frigedagas) m.   Friday
FRIGNAN 3   ask, inquire, learn
FRIGNES (-a) f.   freedom
FRIÞ (-as, -u) m. n.   conciliation, peace,
    security
FRIÞA (-n) m.   protector
FRIÞIAN ii   make peace
FRIÞU (friđa) f.   peace, security
FROD   experienced, old, wise
FRODIAN ii   be wise
FROFOR (frofra) f.   consolation, help
FROWE (frowan) f.   lady
FRUM- pref.   first
FRUMA (-n) m.   chief, leader, man in front
FRUMÞ/FRYMÞ (-as) m.   creation, origin
FRYMLIG   inquiring
FRYNIDIG   desirous, desirously
FUGOL (-as) m.   bird
FUL   foul, impure
FULL a.   full, full of
-FULL suff.   full, full of
FULLAEST (-as) m.   aid
FULLIAN ii   complete, fulfill
FULLWIHT m.   baptism
FULTUM m.   help
FULTUMIAN ii   help
FULWIAN ii   baptize
FUNDIAN ii   attempt, try
FURÞOR   further
FURÞUM av.   even, exactly, just (with verbs),
    just as
FUS   eager for
FYLAN i   defile
FYLCE n.   people
FYLGAN i   follow
FYLLAN i   fill, fulfill
FYLLAÞ m.   fill, plenty
FYLLU f.   fill (of food), plenty
FYLST m. f.   aid, help
FYLSTAN i   aid, help
FYLÞ f.   filth, impurity
-FYNDE suff.   find
FYR (-) n.   fire

FYREN   burning, fiery
FYRHT   frightened
FYRHTAN i   fear, terrify
FYRHTU (fyrhta) f.   fright
FYRMESTA   first, foremost
FYRS (-as) m.   bramble, furze
FYRØRAN i   advance, further
FYRWITT n.   curiosity
FYSAN i   hasten, impel
FYST (-a) f.   fist

G

GAD f.   goad, point
GAD/GAED n.   lack
GADORTANG   continuous
GADRIAN ii   assemble, collect, gather
GAFOL n.   tax, tribute
GAL n.   lechery, wantonness
GAL   happy; wanton
GALAN 6   sing
GALNES f.   lechery
GAMBE (gamban) f.   tax, tribute
GAMEN n.   mirth, sport
GAMOL   old
GAN anv.   come, go
GANG (-as) m.   attack, course, gait, journey,
    pace, way
GANGAN 7   go, walk
GANGPITT (-as) m.   privy
GANIAN ii   gape, yawn
GANOT (-as) m.   gannet
GAR (-as) m.   spear
GARSECG m.   sea
GAST/GAEST (-as) m.   angel, spirit
GAED n.   company, society; lack
GAEDELING (-as) m.   companion, relative
GAELAN i   delay, hinder
GAELSA (-n) m.   pride; wantonness
GAESNE   barren, destitute
GAEST- pref.   guest, visitor
GAESTAN i   frighten
GE . . . GE   either . . . or
GEAC (-as) m.   cuckoo
GEADOR   together

GEAGL (-as) m.   jaws
GEALDOR (gealdru) n.   enchantment, incantation,
    spell; song
GEALGA (-n) m.   cross, gallows
GEANLAECAN i   unite
GEAP   curved, spacious
GEAR (-) n.   year
GEARA   of yore
GEARD (-as) m.   court-yard, enclosure
GEAR(W)E   indeed, readily
GEARGNRYNE (geargnrynas) m.   melting
GEARU   ready
GEARWAN i   prepare
GEARWIAN ii   prepare, ready
GEASCIAN ii   find out
GEAT (-u) n.   gate
GEATOLIC   splendidly equipped
GEATWAN i   equip
GEATWE f. pl.   equipment, trappings
GEAÞ (-a) f.   foolishness
GEBAERAN i   conduct oneself
GEBAERE (gebaeru) n.   behavior
GEBEDDA (-n) m. f.   bedfellow, consort
GEBEDHUS (-) n.   chapel, oratory
GEBIDAN 1   live, live to experience
GEBLAND n.   mingling, turbulence
GEBLEOD   beautiful
GEBOD (-) n.   command, commandment, order
GECNODEN   assigned to, attributed
GECRING (-as) m.   downfall
GECWIDRAEDEN (-a) f.   agreement
GECYND (-a) f.   kind, nature, origin
GECYNDE (gecyndu) n.   manner, nature
GECYÞNES (-a) f.   testament
GEDAL (-) n.   distribution, partition, separation
GEDEFE   suitable
GEDRETTAN i   consume
GEDWOLMANN (gedwolmenn) m.   heretic
GEDWOLSUM   misleading
GEFARA (-n) m.   companion, comrade
GEFERE   accessible
GEFLIT (-u) n.   altercation, contest
GEFRAEGE n.   information, knowledge
GEFRAEGE   famous, known
GEGEARWIAN ii   decorate, ornament

120

GEGN   again, still
GEGNUM   forward
GEGNUNGA   immediately
GEHAST/GEHNAEST n.   clash
GEHEALD n.   custody
GEHENDE   at hand, near to
GEHLAEÞA (-n) m.   companion
GEHLYNN n.   noise
GEHOLA (-n) m.   defender, protector
GEHREOWAN 7   regret
GEHÞU (gehða) f.   grief
GEHWA   anyone, each, each one, whoever
GEHWAER   anywhere, everywhere
GEHWAEÞERE av.   however, nevertheless
(IN)GEHYGD (-u) f. n.   intention
GELEAFA (-n) m.   belief, faith
GELIC n.   similarity
GELIC   equal to, like, similar
GELIMP (-u) n.   happening, occurrence
GELOME   often
GELYND f.   fat
GEMACLIC   conjugal
GEMACNES f.   cohabitation
GEMACSCIPE m.   cohabitation
GEMANA (-n) m.   community; dealings, intercourse
GEMANG (-) n.   assembly, group; mingling
GEMANIGFIELDAN i   multiply
GEMARIAN ii   disturb, trouble
GEMAEC   suitable
GEMAECCA (-n) m.   companion, spouse
GEMAEL   variegated
GEMAENE   common, shared in common
GEMAERE (gemaeru) n.   boundary
GEMEDE n.   approval
GEMET (-u) n.   law, limit, limitation, measure,
    portion, rule, standard
GEMET   fitting, proper
GEMETU (gemetta) f.   pride
GEMM (-as) m.   ornament
GEMOT (-) n.   meeting, meeting place
GEMYND (-e, -) f. n.   consciousness, memory
GEN   further, still, yet
GENEAHHE   often, enough
GENEAHSEN   close, close together, near
-GENGA (-n) m.   goer, mover, walker

121

GENGAN i go
GENGE (gengan) f. group
GENGE customary, usual
GENIP (-u) n. darkness
GENOG plenty, plenty of, sufficient
GENYHT f. n. sufficiency
GEO/IU long ago, of yore
GEOC (-a) f. help
GEOC (-u) n. yoke
GEOCEND m. helper, savior
GEOCIAN ii help
GEOCOR harsh, severe, strong
GEOCSIAN ii sob
GEOFON n. sea
GEOGUÞ (-a) f. youth
GEOLOCA (-n) m. yolk
GEOLU yellow
GEOMOR sad
GEONDÞENCAN i meditate
GEONG young
GEONGORDOM m. discipleship
GEONGORSCIEPE m. discipleship
GEONGRA (-n) m. disciple
GEORN desirous, eager
GEORNE desirously, eagerly
GEORNIAN ii lament
GEOSTRAN a. av. night before
GEOSTRANDAEG yesterday
GEOSTRANNIHT yesterday
GEOTAN 2 flow, pour, rush
GEOXA (-n) m. sob
GEREFA (-n) m. official, sheriff
GERYDE pleasant; ready
GESCEAFT (-a) f. creation; destiny, nature (by
    fate)
GESCOT (-u) n. shot
GESCULDRE f. pl. shoulders
GESENE visible
GESIÞ (-as) m. companion, retainer
GESLIEHT (-as) m. blow
GESPANG n. buckle, clasp
GESPANN n. buckle, clasp
GESPREC (-) n. faculty of speech
GESTAEÞÞIG serious, staid
GESTREON (-) n. acquisition, treasure

GESTUN (-) n. noise
GESUND whole
GESWEOSTOR f. pl. sisters
GESWIERU n. pl. hills
GESWING (-) n. surge of the sea; vibration
GETAESE suitable
GETENGE in contact with, touching
GETWINN (-as) m. twins
GETYNGE eloquent
GEÐINGE (geðingu) n. agreement
GEÞRANG (-) n. crowd, throng
GEÞRING n. commotion, pressure
GEWEALC (-) n. rolling or tossing of waves
GEWIF (-u) n. web of fate
GEWINN (-) n. effort, struggle
GEWINNAN 3 win
GEWISS certain
GEWITAN 1 ascribe, blame; go, die; see
GEWLOH ornamented
GEWRIXLAN i mix
GEWRIXLE (gewrixlu) n. change, exchange
GEWUNELIC customary, habitual
GIEDD (-) n. lay, poem, song, utterance
GIEDDIAN ii recite a lay, speak
GIEDDUNG (-a) f. poem, saying, song
GIEFA (-n) m. giver
GIEFAN 5 give
GIEFEÞE given
GIEFL (-) n. morsel
GIEFNES (-a) f. grace
GIELD (-) n. payment
GIELDAN 3 pay, repay
GIELLAN 3 scream
GIELP m. n. boast; glory, pride
GIELPAN 3 boast, rejoice
GIEMAN i attend to, care about
GIEMEN (-a) f. care, heed
GIERD f. rod, staff
GIERELA (-n) m. garment
GIERNAN i entreat, yearn
GIERWAN i decorate; make ready
GIEST (-as) m. guest, visitor
GIESTLIÞIAN ii entertain
GIET still, yet
-GIETAN 5 acquire

GIF   if
GIFER (-as) m.   glutton
GIFEÐE n.   fate
GIFRE   greedy; useful
GIFU (-) n.   gift
GIGANT (-as) m.   giant
GIMM (-as) m.   gem, jewel
GINAN 1   gape, yawn
GINN   spacious
-GINNAN 3   begin, undertake
GISL (-as) m.   hostage
GITSERE (gitseras) m.   avaricious person
GITSIAN ii   covet, desire
GITSUNG (-a) f.   avarice
GLADRIAN ii   rejoice
GLAED   gracious; happy; radiant
GLAES n.   glass
GLEAM m. n.   noisy revelry
GLEAW   clever, knowing
GLED (-a) f.   glowing coal or ember
GLEDAN i   make hot, kindle
GLENG (-a) f.   honor; ornament
GLENGAN i   ornament
GLEO/GLIEG (-) n.   joy, music and good times
GLIDAN 1   move, pass over, pass through
GLIEWAN ii   rejoice
GLISNIAN ii   glisten
GLITENIAN ii   glisten
GLOF (-a) f.   game-bag
GLOM m.   twilight
GLOWAN 7   glow
GNAGAN 6   gnaw
GNAETT (-as) m.   gnat
GNEAÐ   stingy
GNORN (-as) m.   grief, sorrow, trouble
GNORNIAN ii   grieve
GNORNUNG (-a) f.   grief, lamentation
GNYRN (-a) f.   grief, sorrow, trouble
GOD m.   God
GOD (-u) n.   pagan god
GOD   good
GODIAN ii   improve
GOLD (-) n.   gold
GOMA (-n) m.   gums, jaws, mouth, palate
GOR (-u) n.   dirt

124

GOS (ges) f.   goose
GRAFAN 6   dig, engrave
GRAM   cruel
GRANIAN ii   groan
GRAP (-a) f.   grasp, grip
GRAPIAN ii   grasp, seize
GRAED (-as) m.   hunger
GRAEDAN i   cry out
GRAEDIG   greedy
GRAEDIGNES (-a) f.   avarice
GRAEF (grafu) n.   grave
GRAEFT m. f. n.   graven image
GRAEG   gray
GRAES n.   grass
GREAT   tall
GREMIAN ii   enrage
GRENE   green
GRENNIAN ii   grimace, grin
GREOTAN 2   lament, weep
GRETAN i   approach, greet, meet, salute
GRIMA (-n) m.   mask, visor
GRIMM   fierce, wild
GRIMMAN 3   rage
GRIN f. n.   snare
GRINDAN 3   grind
GRINDEL (grindlas) m.   bar, bolt
GRIPAN 1   grasp, grip
GRIPE m.   grasp, grip
GRISLIC   ugly
GRISTBITIAN ii gnash the teeth
GRIÞ n.   peace, reconciliation
GRUND (-as) m.   abyss, bottom, ground
GRYMETTAN i   roar
GRYN (-as, -) m. n.   harm; sorrow
GRYNDAN i   sink to the ground
GRYRE (gryras, -) m.   terror
GUÞ f.   battle, warfare
GYDEN (-a) f.   goddess
GYLDEN   gilded, golden, made of gold
GYLT (-as) m.   fault, guilt
GYLTAN i   be guilty, sin
GYLTIG   guilty
GYRDAN i   gird
GYRDELS (-as) m.   belt
GYTE m.   flow; blood shedding

H

HABBAN iii   have
HAD (-as) m.   condition, state
-HAD suff.   -hood
HADOR   clear
HAFENIAN ii   hold
HAFOC (-as) m.   falcon, hawk
HAFOLA (-n) m.   head
HAGA (-n) m.   dwelling; enclosure
HAGOL/HAEGEL (haeglas) m. n.   hail, sleet
HAGUSTEALD (-as) m.   bachelor; young warrior
HAGUSTEALD   unmarried
HAL   whole
HALGIAN ii   hallow
HALIG (-e) m.   saint
HALIG   holy
HALS f.   salvation
HALSUNG (-a) f.   supplication
HALWENDE   healing, salutary
HAM (-as) m.   dwelling, home, manor
HAM   coated
HAMA (-n) m.   coat, covering; torso, trunk
HAMELIAN ii   hamstring
HAMOR (-as) m.   hammer
HANCRAED m.   cock-crow
HAND (-a) f.   hand
HANDGESELLA (-n) m.   companion
HANGELLE (hangellan) f.   a hanging thing
HANGIAN ii   hang
HAR   hoary, old
HASU   dark, dusky; gray
HAT   hot; passionate
HATAN 7   call, be called, name, order, promise
HATIAN ii   hate
HATWENDE   hot; passionate
HAEDRE   anxiously
HAEF (hafu) n.   sea
HAEFT (-as) m.   bond, fetter; captive; custody
HAEFTA (-n) m.   prisoner
HAEFTAN i   capture; fetter
HAEFTLING (-as) m.   prisoner
HAEFTNIAN ii   take prisoner
HAEL (-) n.   salvation; well-being

HAELAN i   heal, make whole
HAELE (haeleðas) m.   man, warrior
HAELEND m.   healer, savior
HAELEÞ (-) m.   man, warrior
HAELSIAN ii   greet, salute
HAELU f.   health; salvation
HAEMAN i   cohabit with; marry; have intercourse
    with
HAEMED n.   cohabitation; coition; marriage
HAEMEND (-) m.   fornicator
HAENEP m.   hemp
HAER (-) n.   hair
HAERE   hairy
HAERFEST (-as) m.   harvest, harvest season
HAERM (-a) f.   wave
HAERN (-a) f.   sea
HAES (-e) f.   command, order
HAEST (-a) f.   violence
HAETAN i   heat
HAETE f.   heat
HAETT (-as) m.   hat
HAETTIAN ii   scalp
HAEÞ m. n.   heath
HAEÞEN   heathen, pagan
HAEÞENA (-n) m.   heathen, pagan
HAEWEN   blue; blue-green-gray; blue-purple; pur-
    ple
HEAF m.   grief
HEAFOD (heafdas) m.   head
HEAH   high
-HEALD suff.   inclining, sloping
HEALDAN 7   hold, keep; rule
HEALF (-a) f.   half, side
HEALF   half
HEALFNACOD   half-naked
HEALL (-a) f.   hall
HEALM (-as) m.   straw
HEALS (-as) m.   neck; prow of a ship
HEALT   lame, halt
HEAN   abject; low (physical and moral); lowly
HEANLIC   lowly
HEAP (-as) m.   band, crowd, heap, troop
HEARCNIAN ii   harken, hear
HEARD   brave, hard, solid
HEARDING (-as) m.   bold man

HEARG (-as) m.   altar; pagan temple
HEARM (-as) m.   affliction, grief
HEARPE (hearpan) f.   harp
HEARPERE (hearperas) m.   harpist
HEARRA (-n) m.   high one, lord, master
HEAÞORIAN ii   confine, shut in
HEAÞU- pref.   warlike
HEAWAN 7   cut down, hew, kill
HEBBAN i-6   lift, raise, raise up
HEDAN i   attend to, heed, protect
HEFIG   heavy; severe
HEFIGIAN ii   afflict
HELAN 4   cover, conceal, hide
HELL f.   hell
HELM (-as) m.   helmet; protection, protector
HELMAN/HYLMAN i   cover with a helmet
HELMIAN ii   cover with a helmet
HELP (-as, -a) m. f.   help, support
HELPAN 3   help
HELPEND (-) m.   helper
HENDAN i   hold in the hand
-HENGE suff.   inclined to
HENGEST (-as) m.   horse, stallion
HEODAEG a. av.   today
HEOFAN i-7   grieve, lament
HEOFON (-as) m.   heaven(s), sky
HEOFONCUND   celestial, coming from heaven
HEOFONLIC   divine
HEOFONLIC(E)   heavenly
HEOLFOR n.   blood
HEOLFRIG   bloody
HEOLOÞ- pref.   concealing
HEOLSTOR (heolstras) m.   hiding
HEORD (-a) f.   custody; family; flock, herd
HEOROT (-as) m.   hart, stag
-HEORT suff.   -hearted
HEORTE (heortan) f.   heart
HEORÞ (-as) m.   hearth
HEOÞ (-a) f.   interior of a hall
HER   here
HERE (hergas) m.   armed force
HERENES f.   praise
HERETOGA (-n) m.   general, leader of an army
HERGIAN ii   harry, raid
HERIAN i   praise

HETE m.   hate, hatred
HETLEN   hostile
HETTEND (-) m.   enemy
HIDER   hither
HIEG n.   hay
HIEGAN i   carry out, do, execute
HIEHÞU (hiehða) f.   height
HIELD (-a) f.   observation; preservation, pro-
     tection; guardian, protector; fidelity,
     loyalty
HIELDAN i   incline, slope
HIELTAN i   trip up
HIENAN i   abase, humiliate, lower
HIENÞ(U) (hienða) f.   humiliation
HIERAN i   hear, listen, obey
HIERDAN i   harden, make bold
HIERDE (hierdas) m.   herdsman, herder
HIERE   pleasant
HIERSUM   obedient
HIERSUMNES f.   obedience
HIERTAN i   encourage, hearten
HIERWAN i   mistreat
HIEW (-) n.   color, form
HIEWAN i   form
HIEWE   beautiful, colored
HILD (-a) f.   battle, warfare
HILT (-as) m.   hilt, pommel
HILTED   hilted
HIN- pref.   away
HINAN   hence, from here
HINCA (-n) m.   lame person
HIND (-a) f.   doe, hind
HINDAN   from behind
HINDEMA   hindmost
HINDER   after, back
HINDERHOC m.   snare, trick
HINDERLING   backwards
HIWAN m. pl.   family or household members (lay or
     monastic)
HLADAN 6   load, pile up
HLAF (-as) m.   bread, loaf
HLAFORD (-as) m.   lord, master
HLAW/HLAEW (-as) m.   barrow, burial mound, tum-
     ulus
HLAEDER (hlaedra) f.   ladder

HLAEFDIGE (hlaefdigan) f.   lady of the house,
    mistress
HLAEG n.   derision
HLAENAN i   cause to lean
HLAEST (-) n.   burden; cargo
HLAESTAN i   load, weigh down
HLEAHTOR m.   laughter; noise
HLEAPAN 7   jump, run
HLEMM (-as) m.   noise, sound
HLEMMAN i   sound noisily
HLEOR (-) n.   cheek, face
HLEOTAN 2   obtain by lot
HLEOØ (-as) m.   mountain
HLEOØOR (-) n.   sound; voice
HLEOØRIAN ii   resound, sound out; speak
HLEOW m.   protection, protector
HLID (-u) n.   covering, lid
HLIDAN 1   close, cover
HLIEHHAN i-6   laugh
HLIEP (-as) m.   jump, leap
HLIET (-as) m.   fate, lot, share
HLIFIAN ii   stand high, tower
HLIGAN 1   attridute to
HLIMMAN 3   resound
HLIN- pref.   reclining
HLINC (-as) m.   hill
HLINIAN ii   incline, slope
HLISA m.   fame, repute
HLIØ (-u, -) n.   cliff, hillside, slope
HLOSNIAN ii   listen
HLOØ (-a) f.   troop
HLOØIAN ii   despoil, plunder
HLUD   loud
HLUDE   loudly
HLUTOR   clear; pure
HLUTRIAN i   clean; purify
HLYDRAN i   make a noise
HLYNN n.   noise
HLYNNAN i   resound
HLYNSIAN ii   resound
HLYST f.   hearing, listening
HLYSTAN i   hear, listen to
HLYTM (-as) m.   casting of lots
HLYØAN i   rob
HNAPPIAN ii   doze, take a nap

HNAEGAN i   bown down, humble, vanquish
HNEAW   niggardly, mean, low, wretched
HNECCA (-n) m.   neck
HNESCE (-) n.   flesh
HNESCE   gentle, soft, tender
HNESLIC   elegant
HNIGAN 1   bend low, bow down
HNIPIAN ii   bow the head
HNITAN 1   clash
HNOSSIAN ii   strike
HOD m.   hood
HOF (-u) n.   apartment; court, court-yard
HOGIAN ii   think
HOH (hoas) m.   heel, hock
HOL (-u) n.   hollow (in the ground)
HOL   follow
HOLD   faithful, loyal
HOLDIAN ii   flay, cut up, disembowel
HOLDSCIEPE (holdsciepan) m.   fidelity
HOLM (-as) m.   sea
HOLT (-) n.   grove, wood, forest
HOLUNGA   in vain
HON 7   hang
HOP (-as) m.   wave
HOP (-u) n.   remote valley
HOPA (-n) m.   hope
HOPIAN ii   expect, hope
HOPIG   surging
HOPPA (-n) m.   hopper
HOPPETTAN i   hop, jump
HORD (-as, -) m. n.   treasure, treasury
HORH (horas) m.   filth
HORN (-as) m.   gable, horn, musical instrument
HORS (-) m.   horse
HORSC   lively
HOS f.   company, troop
HOSP (-as) m.   insult, rebuke, reproach
HOÞMA (-n) m.   darkness; grave
HRACE (hracan) f.   gorge; throat
HRANFIX (-as) m.   whale
HRAÞOR   sooner
HRAW/HRAEW (-) n.   corpse
HRAED- pref.   quick
HRAEDLICE   suddenly
HRAEFN (-as) m.   raven

HRAEGEL (-) n.   garment
HRAENAN i   move
HRAEÞ   quick
HRAEÞE   quickly
-HREAD suff.   adorned, clothed
HREAF   leperous
HREAM (-as) m.   cry, scream
HREAW   raw
HREDDAN i   rescue, save
HREFAN i   roof
HREMAN i   exult
HREMIG   exultant
HREOF   rough
HREOH   rough, stormy, severe
HREORIG   in ruins
HREOSAN 2   fall
HREOÞA (-n) m.   covering, protection
HREOW (-a) f.   sorrow
HREOW   repentant, sorrowful
HREOWAN 7   regret
HRERAN i   stir
HREÞ n.   fame, glory
HREÞAN i   exult, glory in
HREÞER (-as) m.   breast, heart
HRIF (-u) n.   belly, womb
HRIM m.   hoar-frost, rime
HRIMIG   covered with hoar-frost
HRINAN 1   touch
HRING (-as) m.   fetter
HRING (-as) m.   peal, ring, sound
HRINGAN 3   ring out, sound
HRISSAN i   rattle, shake
HRIÞ (-a) f.   snow storm
HRIÞIG   storm-beaten
HROF (-as) m.   covering, roof
HROPAN 7   cry out
HROR   active, strong
HROÞOR (hroðras) m.   benefit; joy
HRUNG (-a) f.   rung, spoke
HRUTAN 2   roar
HRUSE (hrusan) f.   earth (material)
HRYCG (-as) m.   back, elevated surface or area
HRYRE m.   calamity; death; downfall, fall
HU   how
HULIC   what kind of

HUND (-as) m.   dog
HUND n.   hundred
HUND- pref.   decade
HUNDNIGUNTIG   ninety
HUNDRED n.   hundred
HUNDTWELFTIG   hundred twenty
HUNEG m.   honey
HUNGOR m.   hunger
HUNGRIG   hungry
HUNTA (-n) m.   huntsman
HUNTIAN ii   hunt
HUNTOÞ m.   hunting
HURU   indeed
HUS (-) n.   building, house
HUSC (-as) m.   mockery, scorn
HUSL (-) n.   host, sacrament
HUÞ (-a) f.   booty
HWA   anyone, someone, who
HWAM (-as) m.   corner
HWANAN   whence, from where
HWANNE   when
HWAEL (hwalas) m.   whale
HWAENE av.   a little, for a little, somewhat
HWAER   where
HWAET (-e) m.   wheat, corn
HWAET   anyone, someone, what
HWAET   keen, quick, sharp
HWAET!   alas!, listen!, lo!, be quiet!
HWAETEN   wheaten
HWAEÞER   which of two
HWAEÞERE   however, nevertheless, whether
HWEALF (-a) f.   arch, vaulting
HWEALFAN i   cover, vault over
HWEARF (-as) m.   crowd, troop
HWEARFIAN ii   revolve
HWEARFT (-as) m.   circuit
HWELAN 4   rage, roar
HWELP (-as) m.   cub, puppy
HWEOL (-) n.   wheel
HWEORFAN 3   move about in circles or sweepingly,
     turn
HWER (-as) m.   pot
HWETTAN i   incite, rouse
HWIDER   where, whither
HWIERFAN i   circle

HWIL (-a) f.   hour, time
HWILC   each
HWILEN   passing, temporary, transitory
HWILUM   at times
HWILWENDE   temporal, transitory
HWINAN 1   hiss, whistle
HWISTLIAN ii   whistle
HWIT   light, luminous, white
HWITAN i   whiten
HWIÞA (-n) m.   air, breeze
HWON av.   for a little
HWOPAN 7   threaten
HWY   why
HWYRFT (-as) m.   circuit
HYCGAN i   think
HYDAN i   hide
HYGD (-u) f. n.   mind, intent, intention,
   thought
HYGDIG   mindful
-HYGDIG suff.   -minded
HYGE (-) m.   intent, intention, mind, thought
HYHT (-e) m.   hope, intent, joy, expectation
HYHTAN i   hope
HYLDU f.   loyalty
HYLL (-as, -a) m. f.   hill
HYNGRAN i   hunger, be hungry
HYPE (hypas) m.   hip
HYPPAN i   mock
HYR (-a) f.   pay; hire
HYRST (-) f.   equipment; ornament
HYRSTAN i   decorate, equip, outfit
HYSE (hyssas) m.   young man
HYSPAN i   scorn
HYÞ (-a) f.   estuary, harbor, landing place
HYÞAN i   plunder, take booty

I

IDEL   vacant
IDELC   empty
IDES (-a) f.   lady
IDLIAN ii   become empty, become useless
IECAN i   add to, increase
IEG (-a) f.   island
IEGLAND (-) n.   island

IELDAN i   defer, delay
IELDE m. pl.   people, humans
IELDE f. pl.   years of one's life
IELDU (ielde) f.   age, old age
IELDUNG (-a) f.   delay
IERFA (-n) m.   heir
IERFE n.   inheritance
IERFNUMA (-n) m.   heir, successor
IERMING (-as) m.   wretch
IERMÞU (iermða) f.   misery, poverty, wretchedness
IERNAN 3   overtake, pass by, run
IERRE   angry
IERRSIAN ii   be angry
IERRSUNG (-a) f.   anger
IERRUNGA   angrily
IEÐAN i   lay waste, devastate
IEÞE   easy; empty, waste
IEWAN i   present, show
ILCA   same
ILCA, SE   the same
ILFETU (ilfeta) f.   swan
IN prep.   in, on
INCA (-n) m.   offense
INN(E)   inside, in
INNA   inner
INNAN   directed inward, inside, within
INNANCUND   coming from within
INNERA   inner, interior
INNEWEARD   inner
INNOÞ m. f.   insides, interior, womb
INTINGA (-n) m.   cause, matter
INWITT n.   malice
IREN/ISEN/ISERN (-) n.   iron
IREN (-) n.   sword
IREN   metal (of iron)
IS n.   ice
ISEN (-) n.   iron, sword
ISERN (-) n.   iron, sword
IU   of yore
IW (-) n.   yew tree

L

LA!   listen! (rhetorical command), lo!
LAC (-a, -) f. n.   gift, offering, sacrifice

LAC (-) n.　play of movement; tumult
LACAN 7　jump; fight; move
LACNIAN ii　cure, treat medically
LAD (-a, -) f. n.　course; support; way
LADIAN ii　excuse
LAF (-as) m.　inheritance, leaving(s), residue
LAF (-e) f.　inheritance
LAGU m.　sea
LAGU (laga) f.　law (legal)
LAM n.　clay; earthenware; loam, soil
LAMA　lame
LAMB(OR) (lambru) n.　lamb
LAMEN　fertile, loamy
LAND (-) n.　area, country, land
LANG　long, tall
-LANG suff.　belonging to; dependent on
LANGE　for a long time
LANGIAN ii　long for, yearn; summon
LANGSUM　long-lasting
LANN (-a) f.　chain, fetter
LAR (-a) f.　counsel, instruction, teaching
LAREOW (-as) m.　teacher
LAST (-as) m.　track, trail
LATTEOW (-as) m.　leader, teacher
LAÐ (-) n.　foe
LAÐ　hostile, loathly, worthy of hate
LAÐIAN ii　invite
LAÐU (-a) f.　invitation
LAÐWENDE　hateful
LAECAN i　spring up
LAECE (laecas) m.　doctor, physician
LAEDAN i　lead to
LAEFAN i　abandon, leave, leave behind
LAEL (-a) f.　rod, strap
LAELA (-n) m.　bruise, wound
LAEMEN　earthen, of clay
LAEN f. n.　gift
LAEN (-u) n.　loan
LAEN- pref.　transitory
LAENAN i　grant, lend, loan
LAENE　on loan, lent, transitory, temporary
LAERIG (-) m.　edge
LAESTAN i　back, carry out, emulate, execute, do,
　　stand by
LAET　slow

LAETAN 7   allow, cause, let
LAEÐÐU f.   harm, offense
LAEWEDE   lay, unlearned
LEAD n.   lead (metal)
LEAF (-a) f.   leave, permission
LEAF (-) n.   leaf
LEAHTOR m.   evil, vice
LEAHTRIC m.   lettuce
LEAN (-) n.   reward
LEAN 6   villify
LEANIAN ii   reward
LEAP (-as) m.   torso, trunk
LEAS (-) n.   falsehood
LEAS   false; lacking; loose
-LEAS suff.   lacking
-LEAST suff.   without
LEASUNG (-a) f.   deceit, falsehood
LEAX (-as) m.   salmon
LECCAN i   sprinkle, water
LECGAN i   lay, place
LEGER (-u) n.   couch, lair
LEMMAN i   hinder, trouble
LENCTEN (-as) m.   spring, springtime
LENDAN i   come ashore, land a boat
LENGAN i   delay; lengthen
-LENGE suff.   pertaining to
LENGIAN ii   ask
LENGÐU (lengða) f.   length
LEO (-n) m. f.   lion, lioness
LEOD (-as) m.   man, person of a nation, prince
LEODAN 2   grow
LEODE m. pl.   people
LEOF   beloved, dear
LEOGAN 2   falsify, give the lie to, tell a lie
LEOHT n.   light, brightness
LEOHT   white (shade)
LEOHT   bright, light
LEOHTE   clearly
LEOHTFAET (leohtfatu) n.   lamp
LEOHTIAN ii   shine
LEOMA (-n) m.   gleam, light, source of light;
    splendor
LEON 1   give, grant
LEORNERE (leorneras) m.   pupil
LEORAN i, ii-2   depart, go; die

137

LEORNERE (leorneras) m.   learner
LEORNIAN ii   learn, study
LEORNUNG f.   learning
LEORNUNGCNIHT (-as) m.   disciple
LEOSAN 2   abandon, lose
LEOÞ (-) n.   poem, song
LEOÞIAN ii   sing a song
LEPPAN i   feed
LESAN 5   pick out, select
LETTAN i   hinder, prevent, slow up
LEÞER n.   leather
LIBBAN iii   exist, live
LIC (-) n.   body, corpse; form
LICCIAN ii   lick
LICETTAN i   make to be like, simulate
LICGAN i-5   fall in battle, lie down, lie down
    dead
LICIAN ii   gratify, cause to like, like , please
LID (-u) n.   ship
LIDA (-n) m.   sailor
LIDMANN (lidmenn) m.   pirate
LIEFAN i   believe; permit
LIEG (-as) m.   flame
LIEHTAN i   brighten, illuminate, light up
LIEHTUNG (-a) f.   illumination
LIESAN i   release
LIESNES (-a) f.   redemption
-LIEST suff.   without
LIEXAN i   gleam, shine
LIF (-) n.   life (biological, being alive)
LIFEN (-a) f.   food
LIFIAN ii   exist, live
LIFLIC   lively
LIGEN   flaming, flashing
LIGET (-ta, -tu) f. n.   flash (of lightning)
LILIE (lilian) f.   lily
LIM (leomu) n.   limb (of a tree, person, etc.)
LIMPAN 3   happen
LIN n.   flax
LIND (-a) f.   linden tree; linden shield
LINDEN   made of linden wood
LIŚS/LIÞS (-a) f.   favor, grace, peace
LISSAN i   subdue
LIST (-as) m.   artifice, cunning, guile
LIÞ (-u) n.   limb, part

LIÐAN 1   go, journey, sail
LIÐE   friendly, gentle, gracious
LIÐIAN ii   become friendly
LOC (-u) n.   bolt, lock; prison
LOCA (-n) m.   bolt, lock; prison
LOCC (-as) m.   lock of hair
LOCCOD   hairy
LOCIAN ii   look
LOF m. n.   praise
LOFIAN ii   praise
-LOGA (-n) m. suff.   liar
LOSIAN ii   escape; lose one's way
LOT (-u) n.   deceit, guile
LUCAN 2   close, lock
LUFIAN ii   love
LUFU (lufa, lufan) f.   love
LUNGRE   quickly
LUST (-as) m.   desire, joy
LUTAN 2   bow down
LYFT (-a) m. f.   air
LYGE (-as, -) m. n.   falsehood, lie, untruth
LYGEN (-a) f.   falsehood
LYRE (-as) m.   harm; loss
LYSTAN i   desire
LYSU   bad, false
LYT   few, small amount
LYTEL   little, small
LYTESNA   almost, nearly
LYTHWON   a few, for a little
LYTIGIAN ii   become guileful
LYTLIAN ii   grow smaller, lessen
LYÐRE   bad

M

MA n.   more
MA   furthermore
MACIAN ii   make
MAGA (-n) m.   descendant, son
MAGAN prp.   can, be able
MAGISTER (magistras) m.   master, teacher
MAGU (maga) m.   kinsman, man, son
MAH   bad, importunate
MALSCRUNG (-a) f.   magical charm
MAMRIAN ii   plan, think out

MAN (-a) f.   intention; lament
MAN(N) (men[n]) m.   man, human being
MAN (-) n.   crime
MAN imp. pro.   one, someone
MANIAN ii   exhort, urge
MANIG   many, many a
MANU (mana) f.   mane (of a horse)
MARTIR (-as) m.   martyr
MAÞELIAN ii   discourse, speak
MAÞUM (maðmas) m.   treasure
MAWAN 7   mow
MAECG (-as) m.   kinsman, man
MAECGA (-n) m.   kinsman, man
MAEG (-as) m.   kinsman, son
MAEGA (-n) m.   son
MAEGDEN (maegdenu) n.   maid, young woman
MAEGEN n.   might, power
MAEGENIAN ii   gain strength
MAEGEÞ (-a) f.   single woman
MAEGÞ (-a) f.   clan, tribe
MAEGÞBLAED (-u) n.   genitals
MAEL (-) n.   mark; time
MAEL   variegated
MAELAN i   discourse, speak
MAENAN i   groan, lament; mention
MAENE   wicked
MAERAN i   glorify
MAERE a. suff.   illustrious
MAERSIAN ii   extol
MAERÞU (maerða) f.   fame, glory
MAESSE (maessan) f.   mass (Christian)
MAESSERE (maesseras) m.   priest
MAEST (-as) m.   mast of a ship
MAETAN i   dream
MAETE   moderate, slight
MAEÞEL (-u) n.   council, meeting; speech
MAEÞLAN i   discourse, speak
MAEW (-as) m.   seagull
MEAGOL   mighty
MEAHT (-a) f.   might, power
MEARC (-as) m.   boundary, mark
MEARCIAN ii   mark out, set up a limit
MEARH (mearas) m.   steed
MEARU   soft, tender
MECE (mecas) m.   sword

140

MED (-a) f.   reward
MEDAN i   take oneself
MEDEME   middling, small
MEDLA m.   pride
MEDREN   maternal
MEDTRYMNES (-a) f.   infirmity
ME(O)DU m.   mead
MEDWIS   dull, stupid
MELD (-a) f.   proclamation
MELDA (-n) m.   informer, reporter
MELDAN i   announce, proclaim
MELDIAN ii   announce, proclaim
MELEDEAW m.   honey-dew
MELTAN 3   disintegrate, dissolve, melt
MENE (menas) m.   necklace
MEN(N)EN (-) n.   maid, slave girl
MENGAN i   combine, mingle, mix; have intercourse
    with
MENIGU f.   multitude (number)
MENNEN (-) n.   maid, slave girl
MENNISC   human
MEOLC f.   milk
MEORD (-a) f.   reward
MEORRING (-a) f.   hindrance, obstacle
MEOTOD m.   God, creator; fate
MEOWLE (meowlan) f.   young woman
MEOX n.   dirt, dung
MERE m.   lake, pond
MERE n.   sea
MEREGROTA (-n) m.   pearl
MERGEN (morgnas) m.   morning, morrow
MERIAN i   purify
MERISC (-as) m.   marsh, swamp
MESAN i   eat
METAN 5   measure (things and distance); mete out
METAN i   encounter, find, meet
METE (mettas) m.   food
METGIAN ii   mediate, mitigate, moderate
METGUNG (-a) f.   mediation, moderation
METUNG (-a) f.   encounter, meeting
MEÞE   tired, weary
MICEL   big, large
MICELIAN ii   grow large, increase
MICELNES (-a) f.   bulk, size
MICGA (-n) m.   piss, urine

MICGE (-an) f.   piss, urine
MICGIAN ? ii ?   piss, urinate
MICGUNG (-a) f.   pissing, urinating
MID with
MIDDANGEARD (-as) m.   world
MIDDAEG m.   midday, noon
MIDWIST m. f.   presence
MIERCE n.   darkness
MIERCE dark
MIERCELS m. f.   mark, target
MIERRAN i   damage, harm, mar
MIERRELSE f.   corruption
MIHTIG mighty, powerful
MIL (-a) f.   mile
MILDE generous, gentle, kind, mild
MILDELIC kindly
MILDS (-a) f.   favor, mercy
MILDSIAN ii   be merciful
MILDSUNG (-a) f.   mercy
MINSIAN ii   diminish, grow less, lessen
MIS(SIN)LIC various
MIS(SIN)LICE variously
MISSAN i   miss
MISSERE (misseru) n.   half-year, summer season,
    winter
MIST (-as) m.   mist
MISTIG misty
MITTA (-n) m.   bushel, measure
MITTING f.   clash, conflict
MIÐAN 1   avoid, conceal, dissimulate
MOD (-as) m.   courage, disposition, mind
-MOD suff.   -minded
MODIG bold, proud, spirited
MODGIAN ii   be proud
MODOR (-) f.   mother
MOLDE (moldan) f.   dust, earth
MOLSNIAN ii   disintegrate
MONA m.   moon
MONANDAEG (Monandagas) m.   Monday
MONAÐ (-as, -) m.   month
MOR (-as) m.   fen, upland
MORGEN (morgnas) m.   day, morning, morrow
MOS (-) n.   food
MOTAN prp.   may, be permitted to
MOÐÐE (moððan) f.   moth, bug, insect

MUNAN prp. remember
MUND (-a) f. hand; protection
MUNT (-as) m. mountain
MUNUC (-as) m. monk
MUR (-as) m. wall
MURNAN 3 bother about, care about, mourn for,
    regret
MUST m. new wine
MUTIAN ii exchange for
MUÞ (-as) m. entrance, hole, mouth, opening,
    space
MUÞA (-n) m. entrance, estuary
MYND (-a, -) f. n. memory, mind
MYNDIG mindful
MYNDIGIAN ii recall
MYNE (-) m. regard for
MYNET (-u) n. money
MYNIAN ii intend
MYNSTER (-u) n. monastery
MYNTAN i intend
MYNTERE (mynteras) m. money-changer
MYRGAN i be merry
MYRGE(N) merry, joyous
MYRGÞ (-a) f. joy, merriment
MYRÞRUNG (-a) f. murder

N

NA never, not, not at all
NABBAN iii not to have
NACA (-n) m. sailing vessel, ship
NACOD bare, naked
NAHT n. naught, nothing
NAHT av. not
NAHWAEÞER neither (of two)
NAMA (-n) m. name
NAMIAN ii mention, name
NAN none, no one
NARD m. ointment
NAWÞER neither (of two)
NAEDL (-a) f. needle
NAEDRE (naedran) f. serpent, snake
NAEFRE never
NAEGAN i approach
NAEGL (-as) m. nail, stud

NAEGLED   nailed, studded
NAEMAN i   deprive of
NAENIG   none
NAESS (-as) m.   headland
NAETAN i   afflict, oppress
NE   neither, nor
NE av. conj.   no
NE neg. part.   not
NE(O) (neas) m.   corpse
NEAD/NIED (-a) f.   necessity, need
NEAH   enough, near
NEAH prep.   near to
NEAH av.   near (at hand)
NEAHWIST m. f.   neighborhood, vicinity
NEALAECAN i   approach
NEARU (nearwa) f.   difficulty, distress
NEARU   confined, restricted
NEARWE   closely, restrictedly
NEARWIAN ii   confine
NEAT (-) n.   cattle, livestock
NEBB (-) n.   beak, beak-shaped thing, bill of a
    bird
NEFA (-n) m.   grandson, nephew
NEFNE   except, unless
NEMNAN i   name
NEOMIAN ii   ring out, sound
NEOSAN i   frequent, visit
NEOSIAN ii   explore, frequent, visit
NEOTAN 2   enjoy, use
NEOWOL   precipitous, steep
NER (-) n.   safety
NERIAN i   save
NERIEND m.   savior
NESAN 5   survive
NEST (-) n.   nest
NESTLIAN ii   build a nest
NETT (-) n.   net
NEĐAN i   chance, risk, try
NEĐUNG (-a) f.   daring
NICOR (-as) m.   sea monster
NIEDAN i   compel, force
NIEDE   necessarily
NIEDFUL   necessary
NIERWAN i   confine
NIETEN (-) n.   small livestock

144

NIEW   new
NIEWE av.   anew, freshly, newly, repeatedly
NIEWIAN ii   begin, happen for the first time
NIEWINGA   anew
NIFOL   dark
NIGOØA   ninth
NIGUN   nine
NIGUNTIENE   nineteen
NIHT (-) f.   night
NIHT f. pl.   days
NIMMAN 4   take
NIPAN 1   grow dark
NIØAN(E)   below, from below
NIØER   below, down
NIØERIAN ii   abuse, humiliate
NIØERHEALD   downwardly turned, inclined
NIØERWEARD   downwardly turned, inclined
NON f. n.   "noon"
NORØ   north
NORØAN   from the north
NORØERNE   northern
NORØMEST   northmost
NOSU (nosa) f.   nose
NOSØYREL (-u) n.   nostril
NOØ (-a) f.   daring
NU   now, now that
NUØA   now (then)
NYLLAN   will not, wish not
NYTAN prp.   not to know
NYTT (-a) f.   use
NYTT   useful
NYTTIAN ii   enjoy, use
NYTTUNG (-a) f.   advancement, profit

O

OF   from, of, out of
OFDUNE   down, from a hill
OFEN (-as) m.   furnace, oven
OFER (ofras) m.   river bank
OFER   av. prep.   across, over
OFER- pref.   excessive
OFERBAEC   backwards
OFERGAN anv.   pass over, traverse
OFERGIETAN 5   forget

OFERGIETEL   forgetful
OFERGIETNES f.   forgetfulness
OFERSLAEP m.   sloth
OFETT n.   fruit
OFFRIAN ii   offer sacrifice (to God)
OFOST (-a) f.   haste
OFT   often
OGA (-n) m.   fear
OHT (-a) f.   persecution
OLAECUNG (-a) f.   cajolery, flattery
OLECCAN i   flatter
OLFAET (olfatu) n.   lantern
OM m.   rust
OMIG   rusty
ON av. prep.   from, in, on
ONBAERU f.   self-restraint
ONCYÞÞ (-a) f.   horror; pain
ONDRYSNE   terrible
ONEGAN i   fear, frighten
ONETTAN i   hasten
ONGIETAN 5   understand
ONGRISLIC   fearful, grisly
ONHAELE   concealed, secret
ONHYRIAN i   imitate
ONHYSCAN i   abominate
ONLAST(E) prep.   behind, in pursuit of
ONSAEGE   impending
ONSAEGEDNES (-a) f.   offering, sacrifice
ONWEALG   intact, whole
ONWEG   away
OPEN   open
OPENIAN ii   open
OR (-) n.   beginning
ORC (-as) m.   cup
ORD (-) n.   beginning; front rank, point
ORETT (-as) m.   battle
ORETTA (-n) m.   warrior
ORF (-) n.   cattle
ORFIERME   lacking, poor in, useless
ORGAN (-as) m.   canticle, chant
ORGANAN f. pl.   organ (musical)
ORGYTE   manifest
ORHLYTTE   destitute
ORLEGE (orlegu) n.   battle, hostility, torment,
    war

ORLEGE   hostile
ORMAETNES f.   excess
OROÞ n.   breath
ORÞANC m.   skill, thoughtlessness
ORWENE   despairing, hopeless
ORWIERÞU f.   shame
OSTRE (ostra) f.   oyster
OÞ   until
OÞER   extra, other, second
OÞÞAET   until
OÞÞE   and, or (strong opposition); until
OXA (-n) m.   ox

P

PALMA m.   palm tree
PAPA (-n) m.   pope
PAEÞ (paðas) m.   path, route
PAEÞÞAN i   traverse
PEA (-n) m.   peacock
PENING (-as) m.   penny
PENN (-as) m.   pen
PIC m.   pitch, tar
PIGMENT (?)   drug
PIL (-as) m.   dart
PIPOR m.   pepper
PLEGA (-n) m.   battle, performance, quick move-
     ment, sport
PLEGAN i   fight, move quickly, play
PLEGESTRE f.   female athlete
PLEGMANN m.   male athlete
PORT (-as, -) m. n.   market-town
PORT (-as) m.   gate
PORTIC m.   porch
PRASS m.   noise, tumult
PREOST (-as) m.   priest
PYTT (-as) m.   hole, pit

R

RACENTE (racentan) f.   chain
RACIAN ii   arrange, govern, rule
RACU (raca) f.   orderly narration
RAD (-a) f.   journey, riding; sea
RAMM (-as) m.   ram (animal)

147

RAND (-as) m.   border, rim; shield
RAP (-as) m.   rope
RARIAN ii   bewail
RASIAN ii   explore
RAECAN i   reach
RAED (-as) m.   advice; help
RAEDAN 7-i   advise; arrange; read; rule
RAEDELLE (raedellan) f.   riddle
RAEDEND (-) m.   ruler
RAEFNAN i   accomplish
RAEFNIAN ii   accomplish
RAEPAN i   tie with a rope
RAEPLING (-as) m.   bound prisoner
RAERAN i   elevate, erect, raise
RAES (-as) m.   attack, battlerush, onslaught,
    rush
RAESAN i   attack, make a rush
RAEST (-a) f.   rest; resting place
RAESWA (-n) m.   military leader; prince
RAEÞ   quick
RAEÞE   quickly
READ   orange, red, yellow-orange
REAF (-) n.   garment
REAF (-) n.   plunder
REAFERE (reaferas) m.   robber, thief
REAFIAN ii   molest, plunder, rape, ravage
RECAN i   trouble about
RECCAN i   care; expound, extend, teach; trouble
    about
RECCELIEST f.   carelessness, neglect
RECED (-as) m.   hall
RECEN   quick
RECENE   quickly
REDIAN ii   arrange, ready
REGN (-as) m.   rain
REGN- pref.   very
REGNIAN ii   establish, prepare
REGNIAN ii   rain
RAINY   regnig
REGOL (-as) m.   canon, rule
RENDAN i   rend, tear apart
REOC   fierce, wild
REOCAN 2   smoke
REOD   red, ruddy
REODAN 2   redden

148

REOFAN 2　bereave; rob
REONIG　mournful, sad
REORD (-a) f.　speech, language, voice
REORD(E) (reordu) n.　food
REORDIAN ii　eat, feast, partake of food; prepare
REORDIAN ii　speak
REOTAN 2　weep
REOTIG　sad, tearful
REOW　cruel
RESTAN i　repose, rest
RETAN i　cheer, gladden
RETU (reta) f.　joy
REÐE　angry
RIBB (-) n.　rib
RICE (ricu) n.　realm
RICE　mighty, rich
RICSIAN ii　rule
RIDAN 1　ride
RIEC (-as) m.　smoke
RIECAN i　smoke
RIECELS n.　incense
RIFT(E) n.　cloak, clothing
RIFTERE (rifteras) m.　reaper
RIHT (-) n.　custom, justice, law, principle,
　　right, truth
RIHT　proper, right, straight
RIHTAN i　straighten
RIHTE　justly, rightly
RIHTLIC　just
RIHTWIS　righteous
RIM (-) n.　count, enumeration
RIMAN i　count
RIMIAN i　enumerate
RIND (-a) f.　crust, rind
RINNAN 3　flow
RIP (-u) n.　harvest
RIPAN 1　harvest, reap
RISAN 1　be fitting, be suitable; rise
RISNE　fitting, suitable
RIÐ (-as) m.　stream
ROCETTAN i　belch
ROD (-a) f.　cross
RODOR (-as) m.　heaven(s), sky
ROF　bold
ROGIAN ii　bloom, flourish

ROMIAN ii   try (to get)
ROSE (rosan) f.   rose (bush)
ROT   cheerful
ROW (-a) f.   quiet, rest, silence
ROWAN 7   row
ROWEND (-) m.   rower
RUH   hairy, rough
RUM(A) m. n.   space
RUM   roomy, spacious
RUME av.   far, far away
RUN (-a) f.   mystery, occult thing, secret
RUNIAN ii   whisper
RYMAN i   clear
RYNE (rynu) n.   magic thing, mystery, secret
RYNIG   good (in council)

S

SACAN 6   struggle
SACERD (-as) m.   priest
SACU (saca) f.   strife
SAD   mournful
SADA (-n) m.   cord, snare
SADIAN ii   be sated
SADOL (-as) m.   saddle
SAGOL (-as) m.   club, stick
SAGU (saga) f.   story, tale
SAL (-as) m.   rope
SALOR (-) n.   dwelling, hall
SALU   dark, dusky
SALWED   blackened, darkened
SALWIG- pref.   dark
SAME   in the same way
SAMNIAN ii   assemble, bring together, gather
SAMNUNG (-a) f.   assembly
SAMNUNGA/SEMNUNGA   forthwith
SAMOD   together
SAMWIST m. f.   cohabitation, living together
SANCT (-as) m.   saint
SANCT   holy, sainted
SAND (-a) f.   meal
SAND f.   political mission
SAND (-) n.   beach, sand
SANG (-as) m.   poem, song
SANGERE (sangeras) m.   singer

SANIAN ii   droop
SAR (-) n.   pain, wound
SAR   grievous, painful
SARE   painfully, seriously; very
SARIG   painful, sad
SARIGIAN ii   grieve, suffer, wound
SAWAN 7   sow
SAWOL (sawla) f.   soul
SAECC (-a) f.   strife
SAED (-) n.   seed
SAED   fed up with, full of, heavy, sated with
SAEGAN i   cause to sink
SAEGEN (-a) f.   saying, tale
SAEL (-e) m. f.   occasion, joy, prosperity, time
SAEL (salu) n.   hall
SAELAN i   happen; tie with a rope
SAELIG   happy, prosperous
SAELÞ (-a) f.   fortune, prosperity
SAENE   negligent, slow
SAEP m.   sap
SAETAN i   lie in wait for
SAETERNDAEG (Saeterndagas) m.   Saturday
SCACAN 6   depart
SCADAN 7   distinguish between, divide
SCADLICE   reasonably
SCADU (scadwa) f.   shade, shadow
SCADWIS   discriminating
SCALU f.   troop
SCAMIAN ii   be ashamed
SCAMU (scama) f.   embarrassment, shame; genitals
SCANCA (-n) m.   shank
SCAND (-a) f.   disgrace, shame
SCAÞA (-n) m.   foe, warrior
SCAECEL (-as) m.   shackle
SCAED (scadu) n.   shade, shadow
SCAEFT (-as) m.   shaft (of a spear)
SCAENAN i   break, shatter; open, wrench; cause to
    shine, make brilliant
SCAETT (-as) m.   coin, money, treasure
SCAEÞ (-a) f.   sheath for a sword
SCEAF (-as) m.   sheaf (of grain)
SCEALC (-as) m.   man, warrior; political minis-
    ter, servant
SCEAP (-) n.   sheep
SCEAPHIERDE (sceaphierdas) m.   shepherd

SCEARD   cut off from, deprived of
SCEARN n.   dung, dirt
SCEARP   discriminating, quick-witted, sharp
SCEAT (-as) m.   corner; lap (of the body); sur-
    face of the earth
SCEAWEND m.   buffoon
SCEAWIAN ii   expose, inspect, look at
SCEAWUNG (-a) f.   inspection; spectacle
SCENC (-a) f.   cup
SCENCAN i   pour a drink
SCENDAN i   disgrace, shame
SCEO m.   cloud
SCEON i   happen
SCEORP (-) m.   clothing
SCEOTAN 2   shoot, shoot forward, shoot into
SCEOTEND (-) m.   bowman
SCIELD (-as) m.   protection, shield
SCIELDAN i   protect, shield
SCIELFE (scielfa) f.   floor, shelf
SCIELL (-a) f.   shell
SCIENE   beautiful, fair
SCIEPPAN i-6   create
SCIEPPEND m.   creator
SCIERAN 4   cut, cut off, shear
SCIERDAN i   damage, destroy
SCIERNICGE (sciernicgan) f.   actress, comedienne
SCIERPAN i   clothe; sharpen
SCIERPLA (-n) m.   clothing
SCIEÞÞAN i-6   harm, injure
SCILLING (-as) m.   shilling
SCIMA (-n) m.   radiance
SCIMIAN ii   shine
SCINAN i   shine
SCINN n.   phantom, evil spirit, spectre
SCINN (-u) n.   skin
SCINNAN m. pl.   evil spirits, phantoms, spectres
SCIP (-u) n.   ship
SCIR   bright, clear, white (shade)
SCIRAN i   make clear; say
SCITTE f.   shit
SCOLU f.   band
SCOP (-as) m.   poet, singer of tales
SCORT   short
SCOT (-as) m.   trout
SCOTIAN ii   shoot

SCRAD (-a) f.   ship
SCRALLETTAN i   resound
SCRAEF (scrafu) n.   cave
SCRID (-u) n.   chariot, vehicle
SCRID   swift
SCRIDE- pref.   striding
SCRIFAN 1   decree, prescribe, sentence
SCRIFT (-as) m.   father-confessor
SCRINCAN 3   shrink
SCRIÐAN 1   glide, stalk, stride (malevolent move-
    ment)
SCUCCA (-n) m.   evil spirit
SCUDAN 2   hurry
SCUFAN 2   push, shove
SCULAN prp.   be destined to, have to, must, be
    obliged to, ought to, shall
SCUNIAN ii   shun
SCUNIENDLIC   abominable, be shunned
SCUR (-as) m.   shot, shower (of weapons); tempest
SCU(W)A (-n) m.   shade
SCY n. pl.   pair of shoes
SCYLD (-a) f.   guilt
SCYLDIG   guilty
SCYNDAN i   hasten, speed
SCYRTAN i   shorten
SCYTE m.   shot
SCYTEL (-as) m.   arrow
SCYTTELS (-) m.   bolt
SEALM (-as) m.   psalm
SEALMA (-n) m.   psalm
SEALMETTAN ii   sing psalms
SEALMIAN ii   accompany with a harp
SEALT n.   salt, salt water
SEALT   salty
SEARU (-) n.   armor; device, machination, treach-
    ery, skill
SEARU- pref.   contrived with cunning
SEARWIAN ii   cheat, dissimulate
SEAÐ (-as) m.   hole, pit; spring, stream
SEAW (-as) m.   juice, moisture
SEAX (-) n.   short sword
SECAN i   seek
SECG (-as) m.   man, warrior
SECGAN i   say
SEFA (-n) m.   breast, heart

SEFTE   gently
SEGEL(E) n.   sun
SEGL (-as) m.   sail
SEGN (-) n.   ensign; evidence, mark, sign
SEGNIAN ii   bless
SEGNUNG (-a) f.   blessing
SEL av.   better
SELD (-) n.   hall
SELD- pref.   remarkable, rare
SELDA (-n) m.   companion
SELDAN av.   rarely
SELDLIC   unusual
SELDLICE   unusually
SELE (-) m.   dwelling, house
SELEST   best
SELF   him, her, or it self
SELLAN i   give
SELLEND (-as) m.   giver
SELRA   better
SEMAN i   conciliate, make quiet, pacify
SENCAN i   cause to sink
SENDAN i   apply (something to something); send
SEOC   sick
SEOFOÐA   seventh
SEOFUN   seven
SEOFUNFEALD   sevenfold
SEOFUNTIENE   seventeen
SEOFUNTIG   seventy
SEOLCAN 3   become remiss, become slack
SEOLFOR n.   silver
SEOLFREN   of silver
SEOLH (seolas) m.   seal (animal)
SEOLOÞ (-as) m.   sea
SEOLUC (-as) m.   silk
SEOMIAN ii   hover
SEON 5   see
SEONAÞ (-as) m.   synod
SEONU (seonwa) f.   sinew
SEOSLIG   distressed
SEOÞAN 2   boil, brood over, cook; cause to well
    up
SEOWAN i   sew
SEOWIAN ii   sew
SEPPAN i   teach
SERAPHIN   seraphim

154

SESS (-as) m.   seat
SESSIAN ii   grow quiet
SET (-u) n.   residence; seat
SETL (-) n.   seat
SETLAN i   seat
SETTAN i   establish, set
SETTEND (-as) m.   founder
SEÐAN i   testify to the truth of
SE ÐE   he who, it which
SEWENLIC   visible
SIBB (-a) f.   clanship, conciliation, friendship,
    reconciliation
SICETTUNG (-a) f.   sigh
SID   extensive
SIDE   extensively, widely
SIEN f.   sight
SIERCE (siercan) f.   byrnie, corslet
SIERWAN i   arm, equip; plan, plot
SIEX   six
SIEXTA   sixth
SIEXTIG   sixty
SIFIAN ii   lament
SIFUNG (-a) f.   lamentation
SIGAN 1   sink
SIGE m.   victory
SIGLAN i   sail
SIGLE (siglu) n.   necklace
SIGOR (-as) m.   victory
SIHÐ f.   sight
SILE (-) m.   hall
SIMA (-n) m.   chain
SIMBEL/SIMBLE(S)   always
SIN- pref.   always, continuous, perpetual
SINC (-) n.   treasure
SINCAN 3   sink
SINDER n. pl.   dross
SINENG (-as) m.   stroke
SINGAL   continual
SINGALA   continually
SINGALES   continually
SINGAN 3   recite poetry, sing
SINNAN 3   care about; strive
SINSCIEPE (sinciepas) m.   marriage
SITTAN i   sit
SIÐ (-as) m.   enterprise, exploit, journey

SIÞ (-as) m.   occasion; time
SIÞ   afterward, late
SIÞIAN ii   journey
SIÞRA   later
SIÞÞAN   after, as soon as, since
SLAGA (-n) m.   slayer
SLAW   slothful, slow
SLAEP m.   sleep
SLAEPAN 7   sleep
SLEAC   false; lazy, slack, slow
SLEAN 6   kill, slay, strike
SLECCAN i   weaken
SLEGE (slegas) m.   blow, stroke
SLIDAN 1   slide, slip
SLIDE (slidas) m.   error, slip
SLIDOR   slippery
SLIEPAN i   put on or off; slip
SLINCAN 3   crawl
SLITAN 1   cut, slit
SLITE m.   bite, cut
SLIÞAN i   wound
SLIÞE(N)   cruel, dangerous
SLIÞE   direly, hard
SLUMA m.   slumber
SLUPAN 2   escape, slip away
SMAEL   graceful; narrow (physically), small
SMAETE   pure, refined
SMEAGAN i   consider, meditate, reflect upon
SMEORU (-) n.   fat, ointment
SMICRE   beautiful, elegant
SMIERWAN i   anoint, smear
SMITAN 1   smear, soil
SMIÞ (-as) m.   artisan, smith
SMIÞIAN ii   work metal
SMOLT   gentle, peaceful
SMOLTE   gently, peacefully
SMEÞE   smooth
SMYLTE   mild, serene
SNAW (-as) m.   snow
SNAED (-as) m.   cut, slice
SNAED (-u) n.   morsel
SNAEDAN i   cut
SNAEGL (-as) m.   snail
SNELL   active, bold, quick
SNEOME   quickly

SNEOWAN 7   hasten
SNER (-e) f.   harp string
SNICAN 1   creep
SNIERIAN i   hasten
SNIÞAN 1   cut
SNIWAN i   snow
SNOTOR   prudent, wise
SNUD   quick
SNUDE   quickly
SNYTRE   wise
SNYTRIAN ii   be wise, know
SNYTRU (snytre) f.   wisdom
SOCN (-a) f.   attack, visitation
SOFTE   gently, softly
SOL   dirty
SOLIAN ii   grow dark
SOLOR (-as) m.   sollar
SOM   friendly, in agreement, peaceful
SONA   immediately
SORG (-a) f.   sorrow
SORGIAN ii   grieve, sorrow
SORGLEOÞ (-a) f.   lament
SORGUNG (-a) f.   grieving
SOÞ n.   truth
SOÞ   true
SPADU (spada) f.   spade
SPANAN 7   lure, entice
SPANG (-e) f.   buckle, clasp
SPANNAN 7   fasten
SPARIAN ii   protect, spare
SPATL (-) n.   spittle
SPAETAN i   spit
SPEARCA (-n) n.   spark
SPEARCIAN ii   spark
SPEARWA (-n) m.   sparrow
SPED (-e) f.   prosperity, success
SPEDAN i   be wealthy, flourish, prosper, succeed
SPEDIG   prosperous, successful
SPELL (-) n.   statement, story
SPELLIAN ii   discourse
SPELLUNG (-a) f.   conversation
SPERE (speru) n.   spear
SPIERCAN i   dry up
SPILD m.   ruin
SPILDAN i   destroy

SPILLAN i   kill
SPIWAN 1   spit, vomit
SPLATAN 7   split
SPLOTT (-as) m.   blot, spot
SPOR n.   course, track
SPOWAN 7   prosper
SPOWENDLICE   successfully
SPRAEC (-a) f.   conversation; judicial verdict;
     speech, utterance
-SPRAECE suff.   of speech
SPRAECFUL   talkative
SPRECA (-n) m.   speaker
SPRECAN 5   speak
SPRENGAN i   scatter
SPRING/SPRYNG (-as) m.   spring, stream
SPRINGAN 3   jump, spring
SPRUTAN 2   sprout
SPRYTAN i   sprout
SPRYTTAN i   sprout
SPURNAN 3   kick
SPYRIAN ii   follow in the track of
STALU f.   stealing, thievery
STAN (-as) m.   stone
STANDAN 6   stand
STAPOL (-as) m.   pillar
STARIAN ii   look at, stare at
STAÞOL (-as) m.   foundation
STAÞOLIAN ii   confirm, establish
STAEF (stafas) m.   staff
STAEFCRAEFT (-as) m.   grammar
STAEGEL   ascending, steep
STAEL n.   place, stead
STAELAN i   establish, found
STAENAN i   set with jewels
STAENEN   of stone
STAEÞ (staðas) m.   river bank, shore
STEAL (-as, -u) m. n.   place
STEALC   precititous, steep
STEALD (-) n.   dwelling
STEALDAN i   claim, own, possess
STEALLA (-n) m.   companion
STEALLIAN ii   take place
STEAM (-as) m.   moisture
STEAP   elevated, high, steep, towering
STEARC   strong, violent

STEARN (-as) m.   tern
STEDA (-n) m.   horse
STEDE m.   place, military position
STEFN (-as) m.   bow of a ship; root, stem
STEFN (-a) f.   voice
STEFNA (-n) m.   bow of a ship; root, stem
STEFNAN i   control, regulate
STELAN 4   steal
STELLAN i   place, put
STENC (-as) m.   odor
STENCAN i   disperse, scatter about
STENG (-as) m.   bar, bolt
STEOPBEARN (-) m.   orphan
STEOPCILD (-ru) n.   orphan, step-child
STEOR (-a) f.   guidance; penalty; steering
STEORA (-n) m.   pilot
STEORRA (-n) m.   star
STEORT (-as) m.   tail
STEPE (stapas) m.   gait, going
STEPPAN i-6   advance, go forward, step
STICIAN ii   stab
STICOL   bitter, sharp
STIELAN i   harden, temper
STIELE n.   steel
STIELED   of steel
STIELEN   of steel
STIELL (-as) m.   jump, leap
STIELLAN i   jump
STIEMAN i   wet
STIEPAN i   advance, elevate, promote (in rank)
STIEPEL (stieplas) m.   tower
STIERAN i   direct, guide, steer
STIERC (-) n.   calf
STIERCED   strong
STIEREND m.   God; guide
STIERFAN i   kill
STIERNE   cruel, stern
STIERNUNGA   severely
STIG (-a) f.   steep path
STIGAN 1   ascend, descend, go up or down
STIHTAN i   arrange, order
STIHTEND (-as) m.   ruler
STIHTUNG (-a) f.   arrangement
STILL   quiet, silent
STILLAN i   become quiet, still

STILLE   quietly, silently
STINCAN 3   move rapidly, rise; stink; whirl up
STINGAN 3   penetrate, stab, thrust through
STIÞ   hard, solid, stern
STOCC (-as) m.   plank
STOFN m. f.   branch, stem
STOL (-as) m.   chair, seat, throne
STORM (-as) m.   attack, storm, tumult
STOW (-a) f.   place
STRANG   severe, strong, violent
STRANGIAN ii   make strong, strengthen
STRAEL (-as, -e) m. f.   arrow
STRAELE f.   arrow
STRAET (-a) f.   street
STREAM (-as) m.   current, stream
STREAW (-) n.   straw
STRECCAN i   extend, prostrate, stretch
STREGDAN 3   fall, scatter
STRENG (-as) m.   string
STRENGEL (strenglas) m.   chieftan
STRENGU (strenge) f.   might, strength
STRE(O)WEN (streona) f.   bed, resting place
STRICAN 1   go, move
STRIDAN 1   stride
STRIENAN i   acquire, get
STRIÞ (-as) m.   strife
STRUDAN 2   disturb, plunder
STRUTIAN ii   strive
STUND (-a) f.   moment, time
STUNIAN ii   roar
STYCCE (styccu) n.   bit, piece
STYRIAN i   disturb, stir
STYRMAN i   cry aloud, rage, storm
SUCAN 2   suck
SUFEL (-) n.   relish, spread
SUGAN 2   suck
SUHT (-a) f.   illness
SUHTERGA m.   cousin, nephew
SUMOR (-as) m.   summer
SUMSENDE   swishing
SUND n.   swimming
SUND   healthy
SUNDFUL   salutary
SUNDFULNES (-a) f.   safety
SUNDOR   apart

SUNDRIAN/SYNDRIAN ii   separate
SUNNANDAEG (Sunnandagas) m.   Sunday
SUNNE (sunnan) f.   sun
SUNU (suna) m.   son
SUPAN 2   sip, swallow
SUSL (-) n.   toil, torment
SUÞ   south, southern
SUÞAN   from the south
SUÞERNE   southern
SUÞHEALD   inclining toward the south, southern
SUÞWEARDS   directed toward the south
SWA   as, so
SWAMIAN ii   grow dark; vanish
SWAN (-as) m.   swan
SWANCOR   elegant, lithe, supple
SWANGOR   heavy
SWAPAN 7   sweep
SWAT m.   blood; sweat
SWATIG   bloody; sweaty
SWAÞRIAN/SWEÞRIAN ii   cease, die out, disappear,
    withdraw
SWAÞU f.   track
SWAECC (swaccas) m.   odor, fragrance
SWAELAN 1   burn
SWAER   grievous
SWAES   beloved, dear; one's own
SWAESENDU n. pl.   feast; food
SWAETAN i   bleed, sweat
SWAEÞER   whichever of two
SWEARD (-as) m.   skin; turf
SWEART   black, dark
SWEBBAN i   put to death, slay; put to sleep
SWEFAN 5   sleep, sleep in death
SWEFEL m.   sulphur
SWEFN (-) n.   dream, sleep, vision
SWEFNIAN ii   dream
SWEG (-as) m.   melody, sound
SWEGEL n.   melody; sky; sun
SWEGLE   brightly, clearly
SWELAN 4   burn
SWELCE   likewise
SWELGAN 3   devour, swallow
SWELLAN 3   swell
SWELLUNG (-a) f.   swelling
SWELTAN 3   die

```
SWENCAN i   labor, toil
SWENG (-as) m.   blow, stroke
SWENGAN i   disperse, scatter about
SWEOFOT n.   sleep
SWEOLOÞ m. n.   flames, heat
SWEORCAN 3   grow dark
SWEORD (-) n.   sword
SWEORFAN 3   polish, rub
SWEOSTOR (-) f.   sister
SWEOT (-) n.   troop
SWEOTOL   clear, evident
SWEOTOLIAN ii   make clear, reveal
SWERIAN i-6/4   swear
SWETE   sweet
SWIC (-u) n.   deceit
SWICAN 1   deceive, give way, escape
SWICE m.   machination
SWICE   deceitful
SWICIAN ii   depart, wander
SWICOL   deceitful
SWIERA (-n) m.   neck
SWIFAN 1   revolve
SWIFT   swift
SWIGE f.   silence
SWIGE   silent
SWIGIAN ii   become silent
SWILC   such
SWILLAN i   rinse, wash down
SWILLIAN ii   rinse, wash down
SWIMA m.   swoon
SWIMMAN 3   float, sail, swim
SWIN (-) n.   pig, swine
SWINC (-) n.   labor, pain, toil, work
SWINCAN 3   labor, toil
SWINGAN 3   beset, scourge; swing oneself
SWINGEL(LE) (swingella) f.   whip
SWINGERE (swingeras) m.   scourger
SWINN m.   melody, sound
SWINSIAN ii   sound melodiously
SWIPA (-n) m.   whip
SWIPIAN ii   scourge, whip
SWIPU (swipa) f.   whip
SWIÞ   strong
SWIÞAN i   strengthen, support
SWIÞE   very
```

SWOGAN 7   resound, sound
SWOL n.   heat
SWOTE   sweetly
SWYLT (-as) m.   death
SYFLAN i   provide with relishes, provide with
    spreads
SYMBEL (-) n.   banquet, feast
SYMBLIAN ii   carouse, feast
SYNDIG   skilled in swimming
SYNDRAN i   separate, part
SYNDRIG   separate, single
SYNN (-a) f.   sin
SYNNIG   sinful
SYNNIGIAN ii   sin
SYNTU (synta) f.   good health
SYPE m.   soaking, wet

T

TABULE (tabulan) f.   table
TACEN (-) n.   evidence, sign, token
TACNIAN ii   betoken, make a sign
TALU (tala) f.   narrative; number, tally; speech
TAM   tame
TAMA (-n) m.   tameness
TAN (-as) m.   twig
TAPOR (-as) m.   light, flame, taper
TAT   happy
TAECAN i   commit into someone's hand; direct,
    instruct, teach
TAECNAN i   mark
TAEFL (-a) f. n.   gaming die; game of dice
TAEGEL (-as) m.   tail
TAEL f.   reproach
TAEL (talu) n.   number, order, tally
TAELAN i   blame, reproach
TAEPPERE (taepperas) m.   publican, tavern-keeper
TAESAN i   tear, wound
TAETAN i   cheer, gladden
TEAG (-a) f.   chain, cord
TEALT   shaky, uncertain
TEALTRIAN ii   stumble, wobble
TEAM m.   descendants, offspring
TEAR (-as) m.   tear (drop)
TELA/TILA   well

TELGA (-n) m.   twig
TELGIAN ii   branch out, put forth branches
TELLAN i   count, reckon
TEMIAN ii   tame
TEMPEL (-) n.   temple
TENGAN i   determine; hasten; join
TEOH (-a) f.   band, company
TEOHHIAN ii   appoint, assign
TEON (-) n.   vexation
TEON ii   furnish, prepare
TEON- pref.   injurious
TEO(GA)N ii   furnish, prepare
TEON 2   draw, pull
TEONA (-) m.   vexation
TEONIAN ii   injure
TEOSAL (-as) m.   gaming die
TEOSU (teosa) f.   harm, injury
TEOSWIAN ii   harm
TERAN 4   rip, tear
TIBER/TIFER (-) n.   sacrificial offering, sac-
     rifice
TID (-a) f.   hour, time
TIEGAN i   bind, tie
TIELG (-as) m.   dye; color
TIEMAN i   beget
TIEN   ten
TIERGAN i   exasperate, worry
TIERIAN ii   tire
TIFRIAN ii   offer sacrifice
TIGEL(E) (tigelan) f.   tile
TIGØ (-a) f.   assent, permission
TIGØA (-n) m.   receiver
TIGØIAN ii   bestow, permit
TIL   good
TILIAN ii   acquire, strive for
TILL (-) n.   station
TIMBER (-) n.   building material
TIMBRAN i   build
TIMBRIAN ii   build
TIMPANA (-n) m.   tamborine
TINCLIAN ii   tickle
TINGAN 3   press on
TINNAN 3   burn
TINTREG (-u) n.   torture
TIR (-as) m.   glory, honor

TIWESDAEG (Tiwesdagas) m.   Tuesday
TO   as, to, too
TODAEG(E) a. av.   today
TOGAEDRE   together
TOGEGNES   against, toward
TOGIAN ii   draw, pull
TOHTE (tohtan) f.   battle, fight
TOLENGE   pertaining to
TOM   empty, free
TORD (-) n.   dung
TORHT   bright
TORN (-) n.   anger, grief
TORR (-as) m.   crag; tower
TOSAMNE   together
TOSCA (-n) m.   frog, toad
TOÞ (teð) m.   tooth
TOWEARD   facing, to, toward
TOWIÞERE   against
TRAG (-a) f.   evil
TRAGE   evilly
TRAHTERE (trahteras) m.   commentator
TRAHTIAN ii   consider, expound
TRAEF (trafu) n.   building, tent
TREAFLIC   grievous
TREDAN 5   step, tread
TREDDAN i   step, tread
TREDDIAN ii   step, tread
TREGA (-n) m.   grief, misfortune
TRENDLIAN ii   roll
TREO (treowu, -) n.   tree, wooden material
TREOW (-a) f.   fidelity, reliability
TREOWAN i   believe, hope, trust
TREOWE   honest, loyal, true
TREOWIAN ii   trust in
TREOWÞ (-a) f.   loyalty, truth
TROD (-u) n.   track
TRUM (-) n.   army, force; foundation
TRUM   firm, secure
TRUMA (-n) m.   base; root
TRUMNAÞ m.   confirmation
TRYMIAN i   arrange; strengthen
TU   two
TUCIAN ii   ill-treat
TUDOR (-) n.   men; offspring, progeny
TUN (-as) m.   enclosed place

TUNECE (tunecan) f.   tunic
TUNGE (tungan) f.   language, tongue
TUNGOL (tunglas, -) m. n.   star
TURF (tyrf) f.   turf
TURTLE (turtlan) f.   turtle-dove
TUSC (-as) m.   tusk
TWA   two
TWAEFAN i   deprive of, hinder
TWAEMAN i   part, separate
TWEGEN   two
TWELF   twelve
TWELFTA   twelfth
TWE(GE)NTIG   twenty
TWEO (-n) m.   doubt
TWEOGAN ii   doubt, hesitate
TWEON ii   doubt, hesitate
TWEONELEOHT (-) n.   evening, twilight
TWEONOL   uncertain
TWIG (-u) n.   twig
TYDERNES (-a) f.   weakness
TYDRAN i   produce (progeny)
TYDRE   frail, weak
TYHT m.   instruction; motion, movement
TYHTAN i   incite
TYNAN i   enclose
TYRNAN i   turn
TYTAN i   shine

Þ

ÞA av. conj.   then, when
ÞACA (-n) m.   roof
ÞAFIAN ii   grant, permit
ÞAGEN   further, yet
ÞAGIET   yet
ÞAN   then
ÞANAN   from there, thence
ÞANC (-as) m.   mind, thought, thinking
ÞANC (-as, -u) m. n.   plan, thought
ÞANCOL   considerate, thoughtful
ÞANNE   then, when
ÞAWIAN ii   thaw
ÞAEC (ðacu) n.   roof
ÞAER   if; there, where
ÞAET conj.   that

ÞE part.   what, which, who
ÞEAH av. conj.   although, however, though
ÞEAHNA   conj.   however, nevertheless
ÞEAHT (-u) f. n.   council, plan, thought
ÞEAHTIAN ii   ponder
ÞEAHTUNG (-a) f.   consideration, council
ÞEARF (-a) f.   necessity, need
ÞEARF   necessary
ÞEARFA (-n) m.   beggar, needy person
ÞEARFENDE   necessitous
ÞEARFIAN ii   need
ÞEARL   severe
ÞEARLE   severely, very
ÞEAW (-as) m.   custom, habit; manners
ÞECCAN i   cover. thatch
ÞECEN f.   thatch
ÞECGAN i   consume, receive
ÞEGN (-as) m.   political minister; thane
ÞEGN (ðega) f.   partaking of, receiving
ÞEGNIAN ii   minister, serve
ÞEGNLICE   in a manly fashion
ÞEGNUNG (-a) f.   service
ÞEGU (ðega) f.   receiving
ÞENCAN i   think
ÞENDEN conj.   while
ÞENGEL (ðenglas) m.   prince, ruler
ÞENIAN i   extend, stretch
ÞEOD (-a) f.   people
ÞEODEN (ðeodnas) m.   lord, prince
ÞEODISC n.   language
ÞEOF (-as) m.   thief
ÞEOSTOR   dark
ÞEOSTRIAN ii   grow dark
ÞEOSTRU f.   darkness
ÞEOTAN 2   howl
ÞEOW (-as) m.   servant, slave
ÞEOWIAN ii   minister, serve
ÞEOWOT (-u) n.   service
ÞERSCAN 3   thresh
ÞERSCWOLD m.   threshold
ÞICCE   thick
ÞICCOL   fat
ÞICGAN i-5   partake of, receive
ÞIDER   there, thither
ÞIEDAN i   join

ÞIEWE   usual
ÞIGEN f.   food
ÞIGNEN (-u) f.   maidservant
ÞINDAN 3   swell
ÞING (-) n.   affair, business transaction, thing
ÞINGAN i   invite
ÞINGIAN ii   conciliate
Þion 1-3   prosper
ÞISTEL (ðistlas) m.   thistle
ÞOHT (-as) m.   mind, thought, thinking
ÞORN (-as) m.   thorn, thorn bush
ÞRACU (ðraca) f.   attack
ÞRAFIAN ii   blame, compel
ÞRAG (-a) f.   time, hard time
ÞRAGUM av.   at times
ÞRAEC (ðracu) n.   throng
ÞRAEFT n.   contentiousness
ÞRAEGAN i   run
ÞRAESTAN i   constrain, oppress
ÞREA (-n) m. f.   calamity, distress
ÞREAGAN ii   rebuke, threaten
ÞREAT (-as) m.   crowd, troop, warrior-band
ÞREATIAN ii   threaten
ÞREOHUND   three hundred
ÞREOTAN 2   displease, tire of
ÞREOTEOÞA   thirteenth
ÞREOTIENE   thirteen
ÞRIDDA   third
ÞRIDIAN ii   deliberate
ÞRIE   three
ÞRIFEALD   three-fold, triple
ÞRINDAN 3   swell
ÞRINES f.   trinity
ÞRINGAN 3   crowd, press
ÞRINTAN 3   swell
ÞRIST   bold, daring
ÞRISTE   boldly, daringly
ÞROHT m.   effort, labor, oppression, pain, toil
ÞROHT   laborious, toilsome
ÞROHTIG   laborious, persistent, pressing
ÞROSM (-as) m.   smoke
ÞROWERE (ðroweras) m.   martyr, sufferer
ÞROWIAN ii   endure, suffer
ÞROWUNG (-a) f.   passion (Christ's suffering),
    suffering

168

þRYCCAN i   crowd, press upon
þRYMM (-as) m.   glory, majesty, power
þRYSMAN i   suffocate
þRYþ (-e) f.   majesty, strength
þRYþIG   powerful, strong
þUF (-as) m.   banner, battle standard
(GE)þUNGEN   prosperous
þUNIAN ii   be proud; be stretched out
þUN(R)IAN ii   thunder
þUNOR m.   thunder
þUNRESDAEG (þunresdagas) m.   Thursday
þURFAN prp.   need
þURH   through
þURHGAN anv.   pass through
þURHSMUGAN 2   pierce through
þURSDAEG (þursdagas) m.   Thursday
þURST m.   thirst
þURSTIG   thirsty
þUS   so, thus
þUSEND (-u) n.   thousand
þWEAL (-) n.   bath, washing
þWEAN 6   wash
þWEORH   crosswise, transverse; perverse
þWERAN 4   soften
þWITAN 1   cut, whittle
þYHTIG   bold, doughty
þYLD (-a) f.   patience
þYLDIG   patient
þYLE (þylas) m.   orator, spokesman, thule
þYNCAN i   seem
þYNCþO (þyncða) f.   dignity, honor
þYNNE   slender, slight, thin
þYNNUNG (-a) f.   thinning
þYREL (-u) n.   aperture
þYREL   pierced through
þYREN   thorny
þYRRAN i   dry
þYRRE   dry
þYRS (-as) m.   giant
þYRSTAN i   thirst
þYWAN i   press

U

UFAN   above, from above

UFANCUND   celestial, coming from above
UFANE   above
UFERRA av.   later
UFEWEARD a.   directed up, upper
UFOR av.   higher, late, later
UHT- pref.   dawn
UHTA (-n) m.   dawn, early morning
UMBOR (-) n.   child
UNAGA (-n) m.   poor man
UNCEAPUNGA   without pay
UNDER a. prep.   in lee of, under
UNDERN m.   midday, mid-morning
UNDIERNE   evident
UNGEBLYGED   intrepid, unfrightened
UNGESCAD   unreasonable
UNGNIEÞE   generous
UNGRYNDE   bottomless
UNHIERE   dreadful, eerie, uncanny
UNHOLD   false
UNLAED   wretched
UNMURNLIC   untroubled
UNMURNLICE   unregretfully
UNNAN prp.   grant, not begrudge
UNNYDLIC   extra
UNNYT(LIC)   useless
UNORNE   honest, simple
UNRIHT (-) n.   wrong
UNSCAMIG   unashamed
UNSCAEÞIG   blameless, innocent
UNSLAW   active
UNSYFRE   impure, unclean
UNTAELE   blameless
UNTRAGLICE   frankly
UPAHEFEDNES (-a) f.   arrogance, conceit
UPP av.   up
UPPAN   above, over, upon
UPPCUND   celestial, coming from above
UPPE   above, up
UPPLIC   celestial, upper
UPPWEARDS   upwards
URIG- pref.   dewy
UT   out, outside
UTAN   about, from without
UTFOR (-a) f.   evacuation (from the body)
UTGANG (-as) m.   anus, excrement, privy

170

UTLAGA (-n) m.   criminal, outlaw
UTON   beyond
UØWITA (-n) m.   scholar

W

WA (-n) m.   distress, woe
WAC   frail, weak
WACE   weakly
WACIAN ii   watch, keep watch
WACIAN ii   weaken
WACOR f.   growth
WAD m.   blue dye
WADAN 6   go, proceed; wade
WAFIAN ii   be amazed, astonished
WAFIAN ii   fluctuate
WAFUNG (-a) f.   spectacle
WAG (-as) m.   wall
WAGIAN ii   move, shake
WAMB (-a) f.   belly, womb
WAMM (-as, -) m. n.   crime; spot, stain
WAN n.   lack
WAN a.   lacking
WAN(N)   pale
WAN- pref.   -less, without
WANA (-n) m.   lack
WANCOL   shaking, wavering
WANDIAN ii   hesitate
WANDRIAN ii   wander
WANG (-as) m.   place, plain
WANIAN ii   lack; lessen, grow weaker, wane; pale
WANN   dark
WANUNG (-a) f.   waning
WAR (-) n.   seaweed
-WARA pl. suff.   dwellers in, nationals of, res-
    idents of
-WARAN pl. suff.   dwellers in, nationals of, res-
    idents of
-WARAS pl. suff.   dwellers in, nationals of, res-
    idents of
-WARE pl. suff.   dwellers in, nationals of, res-
    idents of
WARIAN ii   be alert, wary
WARIG   covered with seaweed
WAROØ (-u) n.   beach

WARU (wara) f.   custody, protection
-WARU pl. suff.   dwellers in, nationals of, res-
    idents of
WASCAN 7   wash
WAÞ f.   going, motion, movement
WAÞOL m.   full moon
WAÞUMA (-n) m.   billow
WAWAN 7   blow
WAECAN i   exhaust, weaken
WAECCE (waecca) f.   vigil, watch
WAECNAN i, ii-6   awaken, be born
WAED (-a) f.   garment
WAED (wadu) n.   ford, sea, wading place, water
WAEDA (-n) m.   wanderer
WAEDL f.   beggary, destitution, poverty
WAEDLA (-n) n.   beggar
WAEDLE   destitute, poor
WAEDLING (-as) m.   needy person, poor man
WAEFAN i   enfold, wrap up
WAEFERSYN (-e) f.   example
WAEFRE   shifting, uncertain, wavering
WAEFÞ(U) (-a) f.   marvel, wonder
WAEG (-as) m.   wall; wave
WAEGAN i   afflict, trouble
WAEGN (-as) m.   cart, wagon
WAEL (walu) n.   carnage, corpse, claughter
WAELAN i   afflict, torment
WAEPEN (-) n.   penis; weapon
WAEPNED- pref.   armed
WAEPNEDMAN (waepnedmenn) m.   male, male creature,
    man
WAER f.   faith, trust; protection
WAER   cautious, wary; conscious; true
WAESTAN i   devastate
WAESTEN (-as, -u) m. n.   desert
WAESTM (-as, -a) m. f.   fruit, growth, plant
WAET   wet
WAETA m.   water, wetness
WAETAN i   wet
WAETER (-) n.   body of water, stream, water
WAEÞAN i   roam
WEA (-n) m.   misfortune, woe
WEALCAN 7   roll, surge
WEALD (-as) m.   forest
WEALD f. n.   control, power

WEALDA (-n) m.   ruler
WEALDAN 7   control, govern, rule, wield power
WEALDEND (-) m.   ruler
WEALH (wealas) m.   captive, celt, welshman
WEALL (-as) m.   cliff, rampart, wall
WEALLAN 7   surge, well up
WEALWIAN ii   roll, wallow
WEARC (-) n.   pain
WEARD(-as) m.   guardian, warden
WEARD (-a) f.   guardianship, keeping
WEARDIAN ii   guard, keep, watch over
WEARG (-as) m.   criminal, outlaw; wolf
WEARM   warm
WEARMIAN ii   become warm
WEARN (-a) f.   refusal
WEARNIAN ii   warn
WEARNUNG (-a) f.   warning
WEAX n.   wax
WEAXAN 7   grow, increase
WEBB (-) n.   cloth, tapestry, tissue, woven work
WEBBIAN ii   plot; weave
WECCAN i   waken
WEDAN i   rage
WEDD (-) n.   pledge, surety
WEDDIAN ii   marry, wed
WEDER (-) n.   storm, weather
WEDLAC (-) f. n.   marriage
WEFL (-a) f.   warp, woof
WEG (-as) m.   route, street, way
WEGAN 5   carry; move
WEL   well
WELA (-n) m.   abundance, wealth
WELERA f. pl.   lips
WELERAS m. pl.   lips
WELIG   prosperous
WELIGIAN ii   prosper
WEMAN i   announce, sound; entice
WEMMAN i   defile, spot
WEN (-e) f.   expectation, decision about, opinion
WENAN i   expect, suppose
WENDAN i   go, turn
WENDAN/AWENDAN i   translate
WENDUNG (-a) f.   change
WENN (-as, -a) m. f.   cyst, tumor
WENNAN i   accustom

```
WENUNGA    perhaps, possibly
WEOD (-) n.    weed
WEORC (-) n.    performance, work
WEORCSUM    toilsome
WEORF (-) n.    cattle
WEORNIAN ii    become weak
WEOROD (-) n.    band, troop
WEOROLD (-a) f.    world
WEORP n.    throwing
WEORPAN 3    throw, throw away
WEORÐ n.    price, value, worth
WEORÐ    distinguished, esteemed
WEORÐAN 2    become
WEORÐIAN ii    esteem, honor, praise
WEORÐIG (-as) m.    estate, farmstead
WEORÐUNG (-a) f.    distinction, honor
WEPAN 7    lament, weep
WER (-as) m.    male, male creature, man
WERIAN i    defend
WERIG    tired, weary
WERIGIAN ii    tire
WERMOD m.    wormwood
WESAN anv.    be
WESAN i    soak, wet
WEST    west
WESTAN i    lay waste
WESTAN    from the west
WESTE    desolate, waste
WESTEN (-as, -u) m. n.    wasteland
WESTMEST    westmost
WEÐE    mild, pleasant
WIC (-) n.    dwelling place, farmstead, settlement
WICAN 1    weaken, yield
WICE/WICU (wican) f.    week
WICG (-) n.    steed
WICIAN ii    encamp
WICING (-as) m.    pirate, viking
WID    extensive, roomy, wide
WIDE    widely, extensively
WIDL (-as) m.    filth, impurity
WIDLIAN ii    defile, pollute
WIELD (-) n.    control, power
WIELDAN i    rule, wield power
WIELL (-as) m.    fountain, spring (water)
WIELLA (-n) m.    fountain, spring (water)
```

174

WIELLAN i   be stirred, well up
WIELLE (wiellan) f.   fountain, spring (water)
WIELM (-as) m.   surge, welling up
WIERDAN i   destroy
WIERGAN i   abuse, curse, despise
WIERGØU (wiergđa) f.   curse
WIERMAN i   make warm
WIERNAN i   refuse
WIERP m.   change, turnabout
WIERPAN i   recover
WIF (-) n.   wife, woman
WIFCUĐĐU f.   cohabitation
WIFEL (-as) m.   beetle, chaffer
WIG (-) n.   combat, warfare
WIGA (-n) m.   warrior
WIGAN i   fight
WIGEND (-) m.   warrior
WIH (wios) m.   idol
WIHT (-a, -e) f.   being, creature
WIHTE   at all
WILDE   fierce, wild
WILL n.   wish
WILLA (-n) m.   pleasure, will, wish
WILLAN anv.   will, wish
WILLSUM   desirable, desired
WILNIAN ii   wish
WILNUNG (-a) f.   wish
WIN n.   wine
WINCIAN ii   shut the eyes
WIND (-as) m.   wind
WINDAN 3   circle, turn, twist, wind
WINDIG   windy
WINE (-as, -) m.   friend, friendly lord
WINESTRE, SEO f.   the left hand
WINESTRE   left
WINNAN 3   struggle
WINTER (wintru) n.   winter
WINTRU n. pl.   years
WIOH (wios) m.   idol
WIOHBED (-) n.   altar
WIR (-as) m.   drawn wire
WIS (-e) f.   reason
WIS   wise
WISA (-n) m.   guide, leader, wise guide
WISE (wisa) f.   melody

WISE (wisan) f.   affair, manner, way
WISIAN ii   direct, point the way
WIST (-a) f.   existence; food, meal, subsistence,
     well-being
WISDOM m.   wisdom
WITA (-n) m.   councillor
WITAN prp.   know
WITE (-) n.   punishment
WITEGDOM (-as) m.   prophecy
WITEGIAN ii   prophesy
WITGA (-n) m.   prophet
WITIAN ii   arrange, destine
WITNIAN ii   punish
WITOD   certain; fated to die
WITODLICE   certainly
WITT n.   consciousness, intelligence
WITTIG   conscious, sensible, wise
WIÞ   against
WIÞER- pref.   against
WIÞMETENNES (-a) f.   comparison
WLACU   cool, tepid
WLANC   proud
WLENCU (wlenca) f.   pride
WLITA (-n) m.   face
WLITAN 1   look
WLITE (-) m.   beauty, countenance
WLITIG   beautiful
WLITIGIAN ii   become beautiful
WLOH (-) n.   fringe of a garment
WOCOR f.   offspring, progeny
WOD   beserk, mad, wildly enraged, raging
WODDOR (-) n.   throat
WODNESDAEG (Wodnesdagas) m.   Wednesday
WOH   crooked
WOL m.   sickness
WOLCEN (wolcnas, wolcu) m. n.   cloud
WOM m.   noise
WOMA (-n) m.   noise
WOP (-as) m.   weeping
WOPIG   lamenting
WORD (-) n.   utterance, word
WORIAN ii   crumble, roll
WORN (-as) m.   large number of
WORPIAN ii   throw
WOS n.   juice, sap

WOÐ (-a) f.   noise
WRACU (wraca) f.   pain, persecution
WRANG   crooked
WRASEN (wrasna) f.   bond, fetter
WRAÐ   fierce, hostile
WRAÐE   angrily
WRAÐU f.   prop, support
WRAEC (-u) n.   misery, revenge
WRAED (-a) f.   wreath
WRAENES f.   wantonness
WRAEST   excellent, firm, strong
WRAESTAN i   bend, twist
WRAESTE   excellently, firmly, strongly
WRAETT (-as) m.   ornament
WRAEÐ (-a) f.   wreath
WRECAN 5   drive; recite; revenge
WRECCA (-n) m.   exile, refugee; warrior
WRECCAN i   arouse, waken
WREGAN i   excite, stir up
WRENA (-n) m.   habit
WRENC (-as) m.   ruse, trick
WRENCAN i   plot, twist, wrench
WREON i   cover, hide
WREÐIAN ii   prop up, support, sustain
WRIGELS (-) n.   covering, veil
WRIT (-u) n.   scripture, written document
WRITAN 1   inscribe, scratch, write
WRITERE (writeras) m.   scribe, writer
WRIÐA (-n) m.   ring, wreath
WRIÐAN 1   tie up, twist
WRIXL (-a) f.   exchange
WRIXLAN i   change, exchange
WROHT (-a) f.   strife
WROTAN 7   root up
WUDIG   wooded, woody
WUDU (wuda) m.   wood, woods
WUDUWE (wudewan) f.   widow
WULDOR (-) n.   glory
WULDRIAN ii   glorify
WULF (-as) m.   wolf
WULL f.   wool
WUNA (-n) m.   custom
WUND (-a) f.   wound
WUND   wounded
WUNDIAN ii   wound

WUNDOR (-) n.   marvel, miracle
WUNDRIAN ii   marvel at, wonder
WUNDRUNG (-a) f.   astonsihment
WUNIAN ii   be accustomed to; dwell, remain
WUNUNG (-a) f.   dwelling place
WURMA (-n) m.   purple dye; purple periwinkle
WYLF (-a) f.   she-wolf
WYLFEN   cruel, wolfish
WYNN (-a) f.   bliss, joy
WYRCAN i   effect, fashion, make
WYRD (-e) f.   destiny, event, fate
-WYRDE suff.   spoken
WYRHT (-a, -) f. n.   desert
WYRHT (-a, -) f. n.   work
WYRHTA (-n) m.   craftsman, worker
WYRM (-as) m.   dragon, reptile, serpent, snake,
     worm
WYRT (-a) f.   herb, plant, vegetable
WYSCAN i   wish

Y Z

YFEL   bad, evil, inferior
YFELIAN ii   injure
YMB(E)   about, around, on account of
YMBGAN anv.   surround
YMEN (-as) m.   hymn
YPPAN i   open up
YPPE   manifest, open
YPPLEN (-u) n.   height, top
YSLE (yslan) f.   spark
YSOPE f.   hyssop
YST (-a) f.   storm
YSTAN i   rage, storm
YSTIG   stormy
YÞ (-a) f.   wave
YÞIAN ii   billow, fluctuate
ZEFFERUS m.   zephyr